It's Not Yours 'Til You Like It
H.C. Prange Company- A Sheboygan Institution

Copyright © 2011 by Sheboygan County Historical Research Center

All rights reserved. No portion of this book may be reproduced or transmitted in any form or by any means, electronic or mechanical, including photocopying, recording or by an information storage and retrieval system without written permission from the publisher. Reviewers may quote brief passages in a review to be printed in a magazine, newspaper or on the Web. For information please contact the Sheboygan County Historical Research Center, 518 Water Street, Sheboygan Falls, Wisconsin, 53085.

PRINTED IN THE UNITED STATES OF AMERICA

Second edition published 2011.

ISBN 978-0-9818974-7-9

For information, please contact:
Sheboygan County Historical Research Center
518 Water Street
Sheboygan Falls, WI 53085
Website: schrc.org
Phone: 920.467.4667
Email: schrc@att.net

Table of Contents

Introduction	5
The Prange Family	7
The Beginning of an Institution– The Founders	9
The First Customers	12
The Making of A Big Store	20
Four Stories of Success	31
The Beginning of the End	91
The End of An Era	106
The Final Chapter	110
Memories	111
Recipes	147
Notes and Personal Memories	149

Thanks to friends for allowing us to use their words and their resources, especially John Werner and his *Sheboygan Press*.

Special thanks to all who donated information for this book.

Introduction

Mention the name Prange's and no matter your age from 40 to 90 you probably have personal memories of the legendary Sheboygan department store. Whether those memories are of the annual animated Christmas window displays and caramel corn, the use of due bills, charge-a-plates, layaways, will-call, the x-ray machine in the shoe department or the escalators, they are shared by many and are part of the cherished collective history of the H.C. Prange Company.

This publication is by no means a comprehensive history of the H.C. Prange Company. It is more a trip down memory lane, filled with images, stories and recipes submitted by former employees and loyal shoppers. The story is further enhanced by clips from Prange Company publications, old newspaper articles and images, along with just enough original text to connect the pieces and tell a good story. There are so many stories it's impossible to tell them all so we have chosen to document some of the happenings of the company from its beginning in 1887 to the old store's demise in 1983.

Prange's continued on for a number of years after 1983 before it was sold to Younkers, but in a different building and in a different way. The era of the giant "H.C. Prange family" and the big city store in a small town was over. But what a life and influence it had! Enjoy the memories.

A summer outing for H.C. Prange employees at Black River south of the city of Sheboygan, circa 1910.

Sheboygan Press 1934

H. C. Prange Co.

Shop For The Children Tomorrow —National Children's Day

Kaynee Wash Suits
$1.95 $2.98 $3.50

The new styles for summer are here. Oliver Twist models made from Palmer linens, chambray, twill and fancy linens. For quality there is no finer wash suit made than Kaynee.

Boys' Sailor Suits
2.69 and 2.98

Made of white twill with the navy blue trimmings. Each suit comes with one pair of long pants and one pair of shorts. Just the thing for summer dress and play wear. See them tomorrow.

Sale Flying Suits, 98c
Reproduced from the famous Lindberg flying suit with the American Eagle emblem. Made to retail regularly at $1.25.

Boys' Sport Blouses, 79c and 97c
Boys' Washable Pants, 98c and $1.69

Boy's Section — 2nd Floor

Special F. O. E. Convention Dinner
Tomorrow Saturday **50c** 11 A.M. To 7 P.M.

Roast Veal With Dressing
Mashed Potatoes Brown Gravy
Creamed Carrots and Peas
Strawberry Shortcake
Bread and Butter
Milk

4th FLOOR RESTAURANT

Children's Tams
In Great Variety
25c to $1.98

Tams are the smart millinery modes for children this summer. Flannel tams may be had in khaki, navy and tan at 25c ... crocheted tams with knitted elastic bands in red, white, lavender and navy are $1 ... genuine French Berets in navy, black, tan, copen and red are $1.75 ... beautiful white tams are $1.98. There is a complete range of sizes to select from.

TAMS IN HIGH SCHOOL COLORS
Made of pieced striped felt in various colors including combinations of white and red, Sheboygan High School colors. Very smart for summer. **1.25**

Millinery — 2nd Floor

Children's Sun Suits
39c to $1.98

Give your children every advantage of summer sunshine and its health building rays with one of these sun suits. There are many different styles of English, Broadcloth, Ginghams and Silk and Wool Jerseys. Some of them are smartly trimmed with contrasting materials and others come in fancy stripes and checks.

Infants' Section — 2nd Floor

Children's Coats Reduced.
Now is the time to buy the children's coats for they are all being sold at great reductions. All sizes and many different styles are especially low priced.

Candy Specials
Denver Sand. Bars
Baby Ruth Bars
Oh. Henry Bars **37c**
Milky Way Bars **Doz.**
Hershey Bars

Beechnut Mints, Beechnut Wintergreen, Beechnut Limes, Roll **3c**

Beechnut Candy Drops, Roll 3c
Halloway Suckers, 4c; 3 for 10c
Black Cow Suckers, 4c; 3 for 10c
Tulip Tart Suckers, 3 for 2c
Licorice Suckers, 3 for 2c
Butter Suckers, Only 3 for 2c

Pure Food Grocery

Girls' Ensemble Dresses
$1.69 to $5.00

Ensemble dresses of pique, prints and linen are just as popular with the younger miss as with her mother. The dresses are sleeveless and trimmed to match the coat and the coats are long. Sizes 7 to 14.

Pretty 1-piece Frocks
$1.50 to $3.98

Smartly made of dimities, piques and voiles in sleeveless and short sleeve styles. They have large scalloped collars and square and round necks with trimmings to match.

House Dresses — 2nd Floor

Misses' and Children's Sport Oxfords

Sizes 8½ to 2
2.69 to 2.98

Genuine crepe soles with tan calf sport elk trimming. A smart and serviceable oxford that is very moderately priced. Made on the correct lasts for children.

Children's Play Oxfords
They come with good quality leather soles and rubber heels and the sizes are from 8½ to 11. **$1.23**

Shoes — Main Floor

Sheboygan Press 1927

WEDNESDAY, AUGUST 10, 1927

August Delineators Are Here—Call For Yours At Pattern Dept.

H. C. Prange Co.
SHEBOYGAN'S LARGEST DEPARTMENT STORE

Once a Fur Coat is sold, our interest in it does not cease. We have available for your convenience a fully equipped modern cold storage and repair service.

We strongly recommend that you avail yourself of this Cold Storage and Repair Service, for by proper care the life of a Fur garment is greatly prolonged.

Now In Progress—Our August
SALE of FURS
Lowest Prices of the Year
Reductions up to 20%

Presenting a most complete assortment of the authentic few Fur Fashions for the coming season. Now is the time to make your selection.

SMART STYLES — CHOICE PELTS

Buy Now!
—Better quality skins and more careful workmanship.
—Longer seasons wear.
—Ready for wear on first cold evenings.
—Largest assortments.
—Lower prices than later.

A Deposit Reserves Your Selection
A nominal deposit of 10% will reserve your garment during this sale. Free Cold Storage and Insurance until your coat is wanted in Fall.

The Selections are now at their Best
You will find the Pelts used of the very best quality, the pick of the season's catch, and the workmanship is much better than is found in the coats made up later during the rush season.

The New Fur Styles for this Season
We show every fashion favored in furs. Furs for Sport wear and Furs for Dress wear. Featuring the newest sleeve and collar treatments and new designs of exquisite silk linings. Also many new novelty trimmings.

Fine Hudson Seal Coats
The choicest Hudson Seal (Dyed Muskrat) skins, selected for their softness and lustre. Trimmed with Skunk, American Mink, Squirrel, all shades, Fitch and Beaver. All sumptuously silk lined. Regular and extra sizes. Missy and Matron models. Priced at—
$280.00 to $490.00

Popular Sealene Coats
A beautiful collection of selected Pelts, luxuriously trimmed with Squirrel, all shades, Skunk, American Mink, Fitch, Natural and Dyed Fox, Ermine, Calf, Opossum, etc. Unequalled values. All sizes, styles for everybody.
$99.00 to $245.00

Mendoza Beaver Coats
Mendoza Beaver (Coney-Beaver Dyed), is becoming more popular each season due to its being a good wearing, popular priced, rich-looking fur. We show them in Tomboy models and also trimmed with Fox, Squirrel and Leather. Exceptional values. Priced at—
$60.00 to $161.00

Pony Coats— Smartly Trimmed
A collection of smart Sport Coats, of Natural Blonde, Taupe, Black and Brown Pony. Beautifully sported, trimmed with silky Fox, Beaver, Nutria, Otter and Fitch. Fancy silk linings. Priced at—
$120.00 to $280.00

Raccoon Sport Coats
Swagger Tomboy model Raccoon Coats, with deep cuffs and double furred Tomboy collars. Only fine, full furred richly colored skins are used, and you will get unlimited satisfaction from one of these durable, smart Sport Coats. Priced at—
$259.00 to $399.00

Fox Trimmed Caracul Coats
Superior quality, full sized, solid skins, of Brown Caracul — trimmed with fluffy, full furred collars of Brown Fox in crusher and shawl collar styles. All handsomely silk lined. Extra values. Priced at—
$100.00 to $161.00

Durable Muskrat Coats
Each one of these style-correct Coats are a model of extreme smartness, featured in Northern and Southern Muskrats. All beautifully lined in plain styles and trimmed with contrasting furs of Fox, Skunk, Natural and Dyed; and Beaver. Priced at—
$206.00 to $280.00

Stylish Silver Muskrat Coats
Exquisite Coats made of choicest clear colored Northern Silver Muskrat skins. Beautifully matched, featuring new long shawl collars and the youthful Johnny collar. Trimmed with Fox, Red and Brown and Beaver. Priced at—
$241.00 to $315.00

American Opossum Coats, Marmot Coats, Beaver Coats, Squirrelette Coats, Am. Broadtail Coats, Wool Seal Coats

Select Early--The best Fur Values of the Year

Prange's Store—Second Floor

H. C. Prange Co.—Leaders of Lowest Prices.—Phone 3600

The Prange Family

The Prange story in America began in 1848 when William Prange, born in Hanover, Germany in 1817, immigrated to Sheboygan County. He married Miss Eleanor Ackermann on March 8, 1849. Mrs. Prange was also a native of Germany, although from Schaumburg. The couple purchased their 160-acre farm located one mile west of the Green Bay Road (now Highway 32) in the town of Sheboygan Falls. They had seven children, the youngest of whom was Henry Carl (H.C.).

When William Prange died in 1865, his wife was left to support and raise seven children. Henry was a frail child who according to his parents wasn't up to the rigors of farm life, and as he approached his twenty-first birthday Eleanor Prange suggested young Henry go to Sheboygan to find a job better suited to his health. And so began Henry Prange's life in retail.

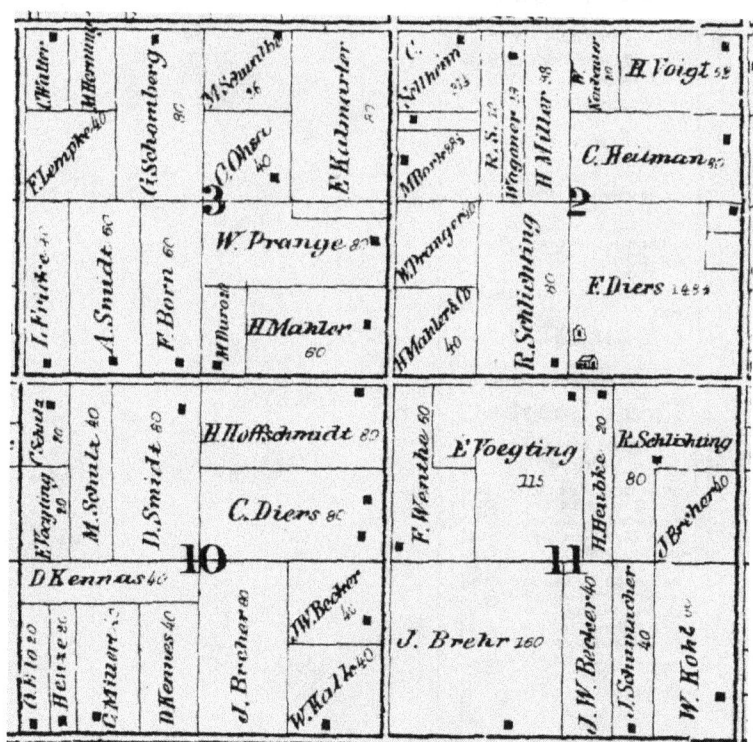

At left is a portion of the 1862 Sheboygan County plat map showing the Prange farm located in section three of the town of Sheboygan Falls.

Below is a description of Henry C. Prange found in the Sheboygan City Directory printed in 1884.

January 25, 1884	City Directory Entry

Henry Prange, age 21 years, head clerk at H.D. Ottens, dark complexion, medium size, trying to raise a moustache, very good salesman, the ladies are very fond of being waited on by him. It being reported that he has tried, with what success we cannot tell, to obtain a matrimonial partner. He will probably fall a willing victim, if not already taken; he has a salary of $1000 and boards at two hotels.

Truthfully Told — Truthfully Sold

| For Picnic Suggestions Visit Our Pure Food Dep't. | **H. C. Prange Co.** SHEBOYGAN'S LARGEST DEPARTMENT STORE | Eat More Cheese We Carry 41 Different Varieties Special Lunch Cheese on hand |

Sheboygan Press 1924

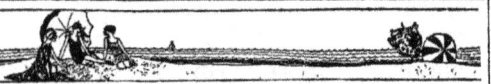

The Most Distinctive Styles In
1924 Bathing Suits
For Ladies, Misses and Children

THE accompanying illustration portrays the very styles now being worn on the fashionable bathing beaches. Designed by style creators of note, who have now given the fair sex a bathing garment that allows for greater activity in the water without becoming fatigued.

Bathing Shoes

Canvas and rubber styles in all shades to match suits. Priced from

25c to $1.39

Bathing Caps

Novelty designed caps in shades to blend with suit combinations. Prices

10c to $1.25

OUR Bathing Suit assortments are not limited to a few, but a generous assemblage including the popular Ocean brand. There are All Wool and Cotton Suits in the season's striking combinations and colors of Jockey, Peacock, Buff, Green, Navy, Black, Royal and Tangerine.

Prices

$1.59 to $11.98

Water Wings

The famous Ayvads wings for the beginner. Anyone can use them. Price

45c

(Prange's Second Floor)

These Beautiful Summery
White and Colored Hats

One Lot at	Another Fine Lot at
$2.69	**$4.39**

Dressy Hats
Tailored Models
Sports Hats
Daytime Hats

This sale of Ladies' Hats presents one of the grandest varieties of the newer shapes in their fullest beauty—dainty summery and ever so attractive.

Hats of crepe, faille and taffeta, also ribbons.

Original models of unusual beauty!

(Prange's Second Floor)

A New Type
Ribbonette Girdle
For the Slender and Average Figure

$2.00 $3.00

$5.00

THESE new designed Girdles by the noted Bon Ton and Royal Worcester makers are a revelation in Girdle comfort. They're the finest combination of lustrous broche and ribbons ever produced. If you want to enjoy summer's comfort for any occasion wear—select a Ribbonette Girdle.

Known as the topless model; long back, short front with elastic panels on each side and four ribbon inserts, some satin and embroidered ribbons across the back. Flesh color only. See them on display.

(Prange's Second Floor)

Picnic Supplies
At Our Usual Low Prices

Paper Picnic Plates—in four, five, eight and nine inch size. Price range 4c, 5c and **6c**

Plain Crepe Paper Napkins, large size. 100 Napkins for **10c**

Wax Paper for wrapping picnic lunches; 80 sheets of 12x15 inch size. Package **10c**

Waxed Paper Cups, 5 cups to a package. Price per pkg. **5c**

Ronsons Magic Sparklers
A harmless toy
23c

Victory Brand Sparklers
Per carton 5c   6 for 25c

Ronson Repeater
A harmless toy for the Fourth
23c

(Prange's New Basement)

H. C. Prange Co.—Leaders of Lowest Prices

H. C. PRANGE   MISS E. PRANGE   J. H. BITTER

The Beginning of an Institution

The Founders

Few would have been able to foresee when partners H. C. Prange, his sister Eliza Prange and brother-in-law, J.H. Bitter opened the original H.C. Prange store on Tuesday, October 4, 1887 that it would turn into a Sheboygan landmark and icon. That first store, located on the southeast corner of Eighth Street and Wisconsin Avenue in Sheboygan, occupied a space of just 30 feet x 110 feet. It was a small two-story building with offices and living quarters upstairs. Louise Rosenthal and John Bertschy were the first and only employees for the first eighteen months when Otto J. Kohl joined the staff.

It was a true family business from the start. For many years Mr. Prange and his sister bought the dry goods, while Mr. Bitter bought the groceries and had charge of the books. Mr. Otto Kohl, who at first devoted his energies to the Grocery Department, in 1891 took over the Ladies' Ready-to-Wear and Men's Apparel sections, which he successfully handled until his death on July 1st, 1920.

> Company Growth— When the original store was organized in 1887 Sheboygan had a population of 16,357. By 1926 it had almost 40,000. The H.C. Prange Company acquired its store in Green Bay in 1927 and the Sturgeon Bay store in 1930 and the Appleton store in 1945. By the 1940s, the Prange Company employed 576 full-time regular employees and many part-time associates between the home store in Sheboygan and the Green Bay and Sturgeon Bay stores.

Henry Prange

After leaving home at age twenty, Henry Prange found employment in John Plath's general store where he spent the next 11 years coloring butter, packing eggs, delivering groceries and learning the business. Hours were long, 7 a.m. to 8 p.m. and even later on Saturdays, 9 p.m.

After working with Plath, the Wieboldt brothers and several other businesses, Henry Prange began his own business in 1887 always keeping in mind the shopper and the need for superior customer satisfaction. This philosophy helped make his business a success from the beginning. Personally greeting everyone who entered the store by name, he would inquire about their families. Those close relationships with customers made Prange's the place to shop. Those relationships were the key to his business success.

Henry married Miss Augusta Bodenstein on December 29, 1891. The couple originally lived on Michigan Avenue, but later built a home at 617 Erie Avenue where they raised their six children. The family attended Trinity Lutheran Church in Sheboygan. Henry and his sister Eliza were generous donors to their church. Gifts from the Prange family paid for the eighth grade addition to the Trinity School. Prange was always interested in civic organizations and was a great philanthropist.

One of Henry Prange's favorite places was his summer home at Elkhart Lake, which he acquired about 1907 after spending many years staying at summer hotels there. The lake property was the scene of many family reunions and company parties.

The Pranges enjoyed traveling especially in their later years when they spent a number of months each year in Florida escaping Wisconsin's harsh winters.

Henry C. Prange died of pneumonia in St. Augustine, Florida on January 25, 1928. He was 69 years old. His son H. Carl Prange took over the store upon his father's death. Under H. Carl's leadership, the business grew from a single store in Sheboygan to a company with twenty-six stores in three states. But, the emphasis on customer service remained; "It's not yours 'til you like it" endured.

John Bitter

John Bitter was born on a farm in the town of Sheboygan Falls and worked as a cheese maker as a young man. He and Bertha Prange, Henry's sister, were married on March 22, 1885. They moved to Sheboygan in March 1887 and in October of the same year, Mr. Bitter began his long career with the H.C. Prange Co., as a merchant and businessman. During his forty-seven years with the company he was a partner, a stockholder and an official of the company. He also served as president of the Madewell Chair Company and the Art Decorating Company, a subsidiary of H.C. Prange. Bitter's chief recreation was playing cards after store hours. His only extended vacation was a trip to France, Germany, Switzerland and the Baltic States in 1927. H. C. Prange and Company was his life.

Mr. Bitter died in May of 1935 at St. Joseph's Hospital, Milwaukee at the age of 72. He was President of H.C. Prange Company at the time.

Eliza Prange

Eliza Prange was born on the Prange farm in the town of Sheboygan Falls in 1862 just three years before Henry, another of the seven children of William and Eleanor Prange. She spent her childhood on the farm, but when her brother, H.C. Prange, began his own business in Sheboygan in 1887, she worked with him as one of the founders of the business. For many years she bought dry goods for the store, never completely retiring. Considered Sheboygan's foremost business woman, she was also concerned with humanitarian efforts which benefitted Sheboygan's citizens.

But, Miss Prange is probably best remembered for the way she died and for what she left Sheboygan after her death. Fatally injured by her own driverless automobile while placing flowers on the grave of her brother, the late H.C. Prange, she died August 12, 1928 at age 65.

The tragic accident took place at 10:15 a.m. on the morning of Sunday, August 12, 1928. Eliza's car was parked on a slight slope in Wildwood Cemetery, when for some reason it started to roll downhill where it veered off the road and struck Eliza as she stood at her brother Henry's grave.

Mr. Adolph Knabe, who was in the cemetery at the time, rushed to the site of the accident. He managed to stop the car by hanging on to one of the back wheels, but Miss Prange was pinned beneath it. Others arrived and Miss Prange was taken to St. Nicholas Hospital by car. But her injuries were too great, and she died less than nine hours later.

The will of the late Eliza Prange was made public three weeks after her death. After making provisions for the care of her sister, Anna Prange, the will bequeathed $25,000 to Security National Bank in trust for the H.C. Prange Company Mutual Aid Society, an organization which helped to defray the cost of hospital costs for employees who were in need of hospital care.

The will also set aside $150,000 for the establishment and maintenance of a second hospital in Sheboygan, but the donation was contingent upon being matched by another $100,000 to be raised by the citizens of Sheboygan. Miss Prange's bequest along with a $25,000 bequest from H.C. Prange formed the basis of funds used to build what would become Sheboygan Memorial Hospital, seen at left in 1931.

That $150,000 donation of 1928 would be worth $1.9 million today.

Mr. and Mrs. William Fiebelkorn of Cascade,
H.C. Prange's first customers.

The First Customers

On Saturday, October 1st, 1887, before the store was officially open, while the shades were drawn and the store filled with lumber, shavings and dry-goods boxes, and the carpenters still busy putting on the final touches, there came a rap at the door. Imagine the surprise of H.C. Prange, J.H. Bitter and Miss Eliza Prange who were busy unpacking goods at the time, when they were met by Mr. William and Mrs. Otillie Fiebelkorn, who inquired in German, "Kann man schon was kriegen?" meaning "Are you ready for business?" Of course, they were ready. The Fieblekorns bought a generous bill of goods — the first ever sold by what is now the H.C. Prange Company.

The Fiebelkorns owned a large farm west of Cascade and traveled nearly 25 miles to shop, quite a distance in 1887. Something caused them to come back time and time again. Odds are that service and quality caused them to become lifelong customers. The Fiebelkorn's loyalty helped the store grow steadily year after year, until it became the largest store in this part of Wisconsin.

In Germany, Michael Fiebelkorn, William's father, had only two acres and raised tobacco. The tobacco had to be loaded onto a push cart and wheeled nearly ten miles to market. When wealthier farmers, who owned horses, passed by the Fiebelkorns on the road, they looked down and sneered at the poorer farmers. This hurt William and his father deeply. This shame was one of the things that helped the Fiebelkorns decide to go to America where they, too, could own horses and land. Once the Fiebelkorns arrived in America they did very well. By 1906, William owned more than 300 acres of land in Sheboygan County and two houses in Milwaukee. He had one of the first cream separators in the county. For power, he used a small treadle-powered unit and then bought a one-horsepower steam engine. He shipped butter to a fancy grocery store in Milwaukee and received 25 cents per pound, more than 11 cents more than if he had sold locally.

This is part of a full-page newspaper advertisement in German touting Prange's superior products. German-language newspapers catered to the large German immigrant population in Sheboygan County.

In the days before World War I, German was heard in the store nearly as often as English. The German colloquial expression, "Down by Prange's" came to signify the high regard of the community for Prange's as the downtown center of the city.

Henry Prange was credited with the large patronage among the people of the city and county. He spent a great deal of time in the grocery entry greeting customers, many of whom he learned to know by name, visiting with them in German.

1887 Grocery Prices

A water pail of syrup— $1.00
Turkish Prunes, 20 lbs. - $1.00
Dried Apples, 20 lbs. - $1.00
Rice, 15 lbs. - $1.00
Labrador Herring, a pail - 75 cents
Creamery butter, one lb. - 27 cents
Bananas, one dozen — 20 cents
Tomatoes, one bushel —- 69 cents
Oysters, select — 45 cents

Sheboygan Telegram, September 12, 1892
H.C. Prange has had a telephone - No. 36 - put in his store. All orders sent in by phone will receive prompt attention.

***Sheboygan Herald* Article and Advertisement**
April 7, 1894

H.C. Prange, that popular and widely known merchant, is enjoying a large trade as usual and a few lines concerning Mr. Prange and his career will not be amiss and will interest his friends and patrons. Mr. Prange's case is an old head on young shoulders as his ideas of mercantile business plainly show. He was born in the town of Sheboygan Falls, April 21, 1858 and was reared on a farm and attended the public school until August 14, 1876 when he entered the store of John A. Plath and Company remaining there over four years. On the first of September of the same year he entered the dry goods store of Wiebolt and later on was employed by Fred Koehn. In August 1881 he accepted a position with H.D. Otten where he remained until June 1884 when he made a trip to Europe and was absent one year. On his return he again entered the same store and it was July 1, 1887 that he severed his connection with the establishment. Shortly after Mr. Prange opened up his store. His business has been on the increase from the start. Mr. Prange commenced with but three clerks and he now employs forty-six. His success has been brilliant, and goes to show what may be accomplished by one having a natural gift for business.

Sheboygan Herald, Saturday, November 9, 1912

A Remarkable Record Shown

Nothing in the History of Business Enterprises Can Equal the Success of H.C. Prange Company. The Firm's 25th Anniversary

… H.C. Prange company had been in business twenty-five years on October 5. It was also announced that the event would be celebrated somewhat later in a manner worthy of it. The celebration came last Saturday by the opening of the great anniversary sale at which in all departments of the large store, goods are offered at very attractive prices. The firm received many beautiful floral pieces from business friends from near and far.

… The announcement of the anniversary sale did not fail of its purpose as the great crowds on the opening day were simply phenomenal. The day broke all records in the history of the Prange store. Although the force of salesmen and sales ladies was increased by nearly 350, it was with great difficulty that the many customers could be served.

In connection with the beginning of the anniversary sale was the opening of the new store for the sale of pure food articles. As is well known a large three-story addition has been erected in the rear of the original structure and this addition is occupied by the new pure food stock. The main entrance for this new grocery area is from Wisconsin Street. As one enters the from the front door he receives a very pleasant impression. … one sees the inviting displays of the baker's goods, including everything in that line including cookies and crackers. For these goods and those of coffee, tea and spices a new system has been installed whereby they are perfectly displayed.

On the right side is a thirty-eight foot table with a marble top. This is the so-called quick-lunch counter at which lunches of various kinds are served. Twenty-four chairs invite people to sit down to lunch. Coffee is prepared in two patent coffee cookers, one with a capacity of eight gallons and the other with one of five gallons. There is also a soda water fountain. Ice cream and other such refreshments are also served. If one prefers he might sit down to a small table. Thirty-two persons can be served at once. Opposite the lunch counter is the candy department in which all kinds of confections are sold. South of this counter is another at which meats and fish of all kinds can be had. The store is provided with a modern refrigerator in which all perishable goods are kept perfectly fresh.

In the rear and middle parts of the large store is the department where meats and cheeses are kept. From there one goes north to the things required in the laundry—soap, starch, etc. Continuing the department one reaches the cereals, rice, barley, sago, etc. and dried fruit, canned milk, dried and fresh vegetables, berries, all arranged to display them to the very best advantage.

To the left as one enters from Wisconsin Avenue is the smokers' department in which the one who loves his pipe can have his wants supplied. Farther along are canned fruits of every conceivable variety and in great quantities. In the rear of these is an art gallery arranged so as to make a very attractive background, while it provides a place for storing flour. Through an electrical apparatus a "lift" is run by which goods are easily brought from the basement to the salesrooms.

Two elevators lead to the two upper stories of the building. One is used to carry people up and down, while the other is for the moving of goods from one story to another.

In the second story are the departments for curtains, shades, draperies, carpets, rugs, oilcloths and wall paper. The arrangements of the goods is such as to make it very convenient for customers to make their selections. On this floor will be the main office with which a fire-proof vault will be connected. The office will not, however, be occupied before the first of the next year.

The third story will be mainly used for storing and for a workshop where curtains, etc. will be prepared. The north portion of the upper story of the old store which was formerly used for other goods such as pictures, comforters, blankets, etc. while the part which was the grocery store will be the sales place of trunks, suit cases, books, writing material, etc. as well as for a part of the men's clothing as pantaloons, sweaters, etc.

Finally, it may be added that in the basement of the new building is a refrigerator where meats and vegetables, etc. are kept. There, also, is the ice machine, which cools the refrigerator, and which provides the cold for the grocery department.

H.C. Prange interior shots— oldest store images circa 1915— at left jewelry and personal items, upper right, furs and women's clothing, at right, dry goods.

Sheboygan Herald

A Fine Emporium
1903

One of the finest if not the finest trade emporium has just been fitted up by H.C. Prange the well known dry goods merchant. From the very small beginning made five years ago his business has grown so it is now the largest dry goods business in the city. It at present covers two floors and the basement of a building 50 x 110 feet which makes a floor space of 16, 500 square feet. The first floor comprises the dry goods and grocery department, the front eighty feet being dry goods and the rear for the groceries. On the second floor the carpet department , which is 30x 50 feet, is found filled with a fine and well selected stock of carpets, oil cloths and window shades. The cloak room is 30 x 60 feet and adjoining the carpet department. In this department is also a good stock of shawls and furs. The curtain and drapery department is in the new south addition and is 20 x 45 feet. These rooms are all handsomely carpeted and the walls finely decorated. The unpacking department is 20 x 56 feet and in the rear portion of the building. The goods are taken to it by an elevator and are here unpacked, checked and marked and then distributed to the different departments. The lighting is done by electricity there being eight arc lamps used during the evening. The shelving and counters were furnished by the J.A. Winter Mfg. Co. The automatic car and carrier system is used. The goods and cash are put by salesmen into a basket which conveys them to an examiner who checks them and sees that they are properly put up and then returned to the salesman. This avoids the possibility of making mistakes. The heating is done with the Boyington hot water furnace which furnishes heat to 18 radiators of which 13 are on the first floor and 5 upstairs.

Sheboygan Herald

To Erect Building February 17, 1909

The H.C. Prange Co. Will Build on the Riedel Property

ARCHITECT HILPERTSHAUSER

To Make Plans For a Three or Four Story Brick Building 40 by 120 Feet With an Elegant Front

The H.C. Prange Co. has taken possession of the property recently purchased from John G. Riedel and has instructed Chas. Hilpertshauser to draw plans for a new building 40 by 120 feet. The new building will be used in connection with the already large department store. The building will be equipped with an elevator and other new and up-to-date accommodations will be placed in the building.

The basement of the new building will be used as a Bargain Basement as in the old store. The first floor will be occupied by the gents furnishing department. The school supply department will be occupied by the shoe department thus making room for the enlargement of the dry goods department. The second floor will be entirely occupied by the carpet, curtain and wall paper department, while the place now occupied by these departments will be converted into the cloak department.

The rear of the third story will be used for the sewing of carpets, picture framing and the making of curtains. The erection of the new building will begin as soon as possible, and when complete the H.C. Prange Co. will have a frontage of 150 feet on N. 8th Street .

From a rather modest beginning in 1887, the Prange store grew and developed a loyal following of customers. The original two-story frame building was used for the business during the following thirty-six years. Five additional purchases were made of land and buildings to complete the frontage on North Eighth Street. As business expanded from that original, long, narrow space, various buildings and additions were built so the store eventually occupied six buildings with extended basements that covered the better part of a square block.

But, by 1923, the business had grown so much it made operating in the old cluster of buildings difficult. The shoe department building was east of the main store, and further east of that was the grocery building built in 1912 with its entrance facing Wisconsin Avenue. These parts were separate buildings divided by heavy brick masonry walls with connecting openings at the main aisles. A row of houses facing Seventh Street lined the east part of the block in those days, and barns for horses and delivery wagons and sleighs were located on the north side of Wisconsin Avenue opposite the grocery department entrance.

In 1923, the original building was razed to make room for a four-story structure. At that time, it was said to be the most modern department store in the state outside of Milwaukee, and the H.C. Prange Co. was well on its way to becoming one of the durable institutions of Sheboygan's downtown. With over 180,000 square feet of retail space it was also the largest department store outside of Milwaukee.

The Making of A Big Store
H.C. Prange Co. 1887-1923
Portions Taken from an H.C. Prange Publication as told by Mr. Prange

How Things Have Changed Since Father Was a Boy

Yes Sir! This is the H.C. Prange Company's new store. Hardly recognized it, did you? Well, Sheboygan has had some wonderful changes since you left thirty years ago. I don't suppose you ever expected to see such an institution in a city of 32,000.

You say you can still recall when we started in business way back in 1887. Let me compliment you on your memory. It will be exactly thirty-six years ago this coming October when this establishment opened for business. How time does fly. In those days the original founders, whom I want you to meet, were the clerks, the buyers, the delivery system — yes, the whole works. Today we have more than 400 employees.

Suppose we take a little stroll through the store itself. I shall be glad to explain to you its various unique features and interesting departments. You will find that the store has not only greatly increased its space, but also its facilities for giving prompt and accurate service to its customers.

> The H.C. Prange Company, seen above in 1903, was situated on the southeast corner of Eighth Street and Wisconsin Avenue in Sheboygan. Notice the display cases protruding onto Wisconsin Avenue advertising kitchen gadgets and toys.

Main Floor

Now for an inspection of our Main Floor. This is the real show place of our establishment. Let's step over here where we can get a better view of the entire floor. May I call your attention to the terrazzo aisle, twenty feet wide, running lengthwise through the store. Notice the counters on either side. These are for the display of specially priced bargains from the various departments.

To the south of this aisle you will find a large and complete department of drug sundries, notions, stationery and books. To the north are located the jewelry, leather goods, ribbons and neckwear, handkerchiefs, underwear and hosiery departments. You will note that these departments are all handsomely finished and equipped with new walnut fixtures.

The eastern end of the main floor may be termed a real up-to-date shoe store where we carry a complete line of women's, men's and children's footwear, from wooden shoes to the Walk-Over and Laird Schober lines. Yes sir, and we also maintain a shoe repair department, thoroughly equipped with modern machinery, where expert cobblers lengthen the lives of worn-out shoes.

In order to insure pure air, we installed a new ventilating system, which changes the air on this floor every fifteen minutes. This makes it possible to continually have fresh, pure air in the store, even though it may be very crowded. This system, in conjunction with the prism lights above the show windows on the north and west sides, makes this an unusually light and airy floor.

H.C. Prange Company was a prolific producer of publications touting the company's place in the retail industry. Publications ranged from items like this 1923 review piece documenting the changes to the new store to fashion catalogues, to employee review and instruction manuals to employee newsletters, all geared to making Prange's "the best" in the industry.

In the early 1900s Model Ts brought farmers and their produce to the H.C. Prange grocery department seen here unloading at the Wisconsin Avenue entrance with its scalloped canopy. Across the street is the livery stable-garage razed in 1962. A mecca for farmers for many miles around, the market provided a hub for socializing as well as the exchange place for the very popular due bill.

Grocery and Farm Produce

Perhaps you can recall our first grocery department, which for eight years occupied only a small space in the rear of our original store. Compare that modest beginning with our present grocery section which now occupies a space of 82 feet by 150 feet. Isn't it a beauty? Let's take a few minutes time to give it the friendly once over.

Yes, we have an unusually large farm patronage. Mr. Prange has always been much interested in the farmers' trade and from the time the store was started has always purchased a large proportion of their produce. This is no doubt due to the fact that both Mr. Prange and Mr. Bitter were born and raised on farms. It may interest you to know that we buy practically all kinds of farm produce such as eggs, dressed poultry, fruits and vegetables that are raised by the farmers in this locality and enabled to furnish this produce to our city customers as nearly fresh as possible and at the minimum cost of handling. Naturally, to properly handle this kind of merchandise requires a large and well-established grocery section.

In order to keep our perishable products in a fresh and wholesome condition, thereby eliminating practically all waste, we have installed a very efficient refrigerating machine that supplies the necessary cold air to the sections where these goods are kept in a fresh, sweet and wholesome condition, so that they will appeal to the most discriminating housewife.

Refrigeration and Fur Storage

Would you like to see our refrigerating plant? As I explained to you before, we maintain a special refrigerating plant in connection with our grocery department, which was established in 1912. The equipment for this cooling system is manufactured by the Kroeschell Company and is a carbonic and hydrite plant. We chose this type in preference to an ammonia system, because it is much safer and free from possibilities of fire or explosions.

This refrigerating system maintains a low temperature wherever needed for preservation purposes. It also serves our refrigerator on the main floor, in which is stored our butter, cheese and meats, each being kept in separate compartments in order to prevent the odor of one affecting the other. This system also provides frigid temperatures for our fruit section, our soda fountain and our special refrigerator on the fourth floor. In the basement a special compartment has been built in which a temperature of two degrees above zero is maintained for the purpose of storing fresh poultry.

This same refrigerating plant also serves our fur storage vault, where a temperature below the freezing point is maintained for the purpose of storing furs. Experience has demonstrated that cold dry air is the only effective method of preserving furs and reviving the lost luster so natural to them. Our storage vaults, which are very popular, are also certain protection against moths, fire and theft.

Yard Goods Storage

This has always been one of our leading departments, and before the store was rebuilt, occupied a very prominent place on the first floor. It has grown to such large dimensions that we have given this department a large space on the second floor.

Notice what wonderful light we have here. This enables us to show the different materials exactly as they are. The spacious floor also makes it possible for us to carry a large stock on display, which, of course, appeals to the buying public, who like to wander among the counters and pick out their patterns with comfort and convenience.

In the Yard Goods Section, occupying a space of 82 x 120 feet, we stock the silks, woolens, linings, wash fabrics, white goods, of this merchandise, as you will notice, is housed on shelves; and the remainder conveniently displayed on more than a hundred tables.

As a convenience to the home dressmaker, the pattern section is located adjacent to one side of the silk department, where McCall's' printed patterns and Butterick patterns are so arranged that instant service can be given.

Ladies' Ready-to-Wear

I know that ladies would be particularly interested in our Ready-To-Wear Department. This Department we opened with a very small stock. Like the other departments, however, it also grew very rapidly, so that in 1909, when we built the four-story addition on Eighth Street, the Ladies' Ready-To-Wear section was assigned a with handsome new fixtures.

This division now occupies the front half of the second floor of our new building and contains several separate rooms where customers can privately look over our many lines of beautiful wearing apparel. To insure our customers the very latest designs in women's garments, our buyers make five to six trips to New York and other large clothing centers each year. We are, therefore, able to always keep our stock in this Department abreast with the times.

The Millinery Department occupies the north side of this floor, where, too, we have arranged several private fitting rooms.

The waist and muslin underwear department occupies the space adjoining the ready-to-wear department, while the house dress department is next to the waist department. South of this section is the corset department, equipped with every modern facility for the privacy and comfort of our patrons.

In the infants' department, next to the millinery department will be found a complete line of infants' requirements.

Men's Clothing and Furniture

The Men's Clothing and Furnishings Department occupies the south 40 feet of the main floor. This department we added to our organization in 1895, up to that time having carried only a very limited stock of men's and boys' clothing and furnishings. Like the other departments, it also always showed a continuous, healthy growth, so that in 1909 when we erected the four-story building, 40x 120 feet adjoining the alley fronting on Eighth Street, the entire main floor of the new addition was devoted to men's and boys' clothing. With the present re-arrangement this department occupies just twice as much space, the floor above having been added to it.

The first floor, as you will note, is devoted entirely to men's furnishings, the second floor to men's and boy's clothing and transferred to the Fourth floor, directly above this one. Much new equipment has been added to this department, making it modern in every respect. We not only sell the "goods" but we make them fit, thus doing all in our power to give perfect satisfaction to every purchaser.

A separate entrance, as well as a separate stairway and elevator to the second floor makes this practically a separate store for men and boys. At the same time, there are openings from the main building to this department, making it convenient for women shopping in other sections to attend to the requirements of their men folk.

The Original Force in the Men's Clothing Department. This picture was taken about the year 1905, when the department was first being firmly established. The eight different men comprising the selling force at the time. They were manager Otto Kohl, Albert Korthals, William Diel, George Fritz, Fred Eckhardt, John Fischer, William Kappers and William Rademacher.

Third Floor

We take particular pride in our carpet, drapery and furniture department, which we shall next inspect. When the store opened we carried only a very small line of carpets, but this department has been gradually increased in size until in 1912 we removed it to the second floor over our grocery department, a space 82 x 120 feet. Early this year, however, we found that still more room was required, so that this department now occupies the entire third floor of our new building, a space 110 x 155 feet.

We maintain several efficient designers to plan interior furnishings of homes and have a modern up-to–the-minute workroom thoroughly equipped with the very latest machinery. We also maintain a staff of men who lay carpets and linoleum, hang draperies and prepare the home for the furniture.

The third floor of our grocery building, a space of 82 x 150 feet, is devoted to a complete line of modern, up-to-date and substantially built furniture from the lowest priced to the best. We are now in a position to furnish a home complete with carpets, linoleum, furniture, curtains, mattresses and beds, as well as kitchen equipment.

The south 40 feet, directly above the Clothing section is occupied by the Art Department and Gift Shop. Here you will find a vast selection of pretty things for the home. The feature of this department is giving free instructions in knitting and making of lamp shades.

Basement

We still have time for a look at the basement. You will be surprised at its immensity. Several years after the opening of the store we opened a house furnishing and crockery department in our basement. From year to year we have added to this department until we now stock a complete line of kitchen equipment, hardware, garden tools, cutlery and crockery. All of this merchandise is conveniently displayed so that customers have no difficulty in looking over our stock and making their selections.

Each year a good part of the basement is transformed into a toy-land, offering a seasonable display for the Holidays.

Let me call your attention to our modern electrical appliance department. Here we have a complete line of electrical appliances, including electric washing machines, vacuum cleaners, and other household equipment.

On account of our excellent ventilation system, shopping in the basement is no less comfortable than in any other part of the store, there being a complete change of air every fifteen minutes. This department can be reached by five elevators and three main stairways.

In the basement we have also arranged a large transfer department where customers,

H. C. Prange livery was located on the north side of Wisconsin Avenue between Seventh and Eighth Streets. The delivery service used horses and wagons or sleighs and trucks to get Prange's products to customers.

Upon completion of their purchases, can procure their packages assembled at one place. We have also made provision for customers to call for their transfers on the main floor. Packages may also be checked here free of charge.

Restaurant on the Fourth Floor

When we built our new grocery department in 1912 we added a soda fountain and restaurant. This department, because of its popularity, has grown to such an extent that we have provided greatly increased accommodations in our new and up-to-date restaurant on the Fourth floor of the new building. Here will be a very convenient place for customers to meet their friends.

Here, in this very light and pleasant room popular priced dinners are served from 11 to 2, while special orders and ice cream will be served at all hours. Four elevators will give our restaurant patrons good service.

Adjoining the restaurant is a large, spacious lounge room, nicely furnished with comfortable chairs and equipped with telephone booths and writing desks. Wash rooms for both men and women are close at hand.

The service kitchen on this floor is modern and sanitary in every respect, its equipment being thoroughly up-to-date. The ice box is connected with our refrigerating system in the basement.

On this floor we have made special provision for our employees' restaurant, which insures them good wholesome meals at moderate cost. Also recreation room, men's smoking room, first-aid room and special instruction room for the training of our employees.

Delivery System

Our delivery system, which I want to explain to you, is a model of efficiency, and consists of twelve horses and wagons, four White trucks, two Stewarts, one Dodge, one Commerce, and four Fords. All this equipment is housed in a modern barn and the adjoining garage opposite our store on Wisconsin Avenue.

This is quite a contrast to the days when one boy represented our first delivery system. He having no delivery equipment, was compelled to carry the packages, assisted on the afternoons and Saturdays by one or two others. Our first horse used for delivery purposes was purchased in May, 1888. From that time on until 1910 additional horses were purchased until we had 23. Then we turned our attention to motor trucks.

Dry goods deliveries are assembled in the Transfer Department by means of a spiral chute in which packages can be deposited on any floor, starting with the fourth. In the Transfer Department they are then properly checked and taken to the lading shed.

The grocery deliveries are assembled in the basement of the grocery department by means of a belt conveyor. In order to avoid all possible errors, all goods are carefully rechecked before delivery.

In order to give our customers the very best of service, we make three regular deliveries each day and, in addition, maintain two extra delivery trucks for service requiring extra prompt and special attention.

Growth of the Store

Thanks to the loyalty and support of the good people of Sheboygan and the surrounding country, the development of the Prange store has been remarkable, it having grown to more than sixty times its original size in thirty-five years.

The store was started in 1887 with a space of 3,000 square feet. During succeeding years the following additional space was added:

In 1889 . . . . . 1,200 square feet
In 1891 . . . . . 2,000 square feet
In 1892 . . . . . 6,000 square feet
In 1895 . . . . . 14,750 square feet
In 1898 . . . . . 3,000 square feet
In 1900 . . . . . 7,500 square feet
In 1902 . . . . . 10,800 square feet
In 1905 . . . . . 11,500 square feet
In 1906 . . . . . 5,000 square feet
In 1909 . . . . . 24,000 square feet
In 1912 . . . . . 41,000 square feet
In 1923 . . . . . 26,400 square feet

This makes a total of 153,150 square feet in the store itself. By adding the 31,740 square feet of space occupied by the Warehouse, Garage and Heating Plant we have a grand total of 184,890 square feet occupied by the store as it now stands.

Prange's Store News, edited and published by and for the employees of the H.C. Prange Company, was issued at the end of each month. The first volume was printed in March of 1925. One article noted that a horseshoe league was being developed for exercise and mood enhancement. The league was organized by Andrew Toutenhoofd.

1926   Fifty Years of Service for Henry Prange

Prange's Store Closes at 11 For Picnic Tuesday

To celebrate its golden jubilee with a three-store employees' picnic at Elkhart Lake Tuesday, the H.C. Prange Company department store will close at 11 o'clock Tuesday morning.

Shortly after the doors have been locked for the day, the entire store personnel with husbands or wives will march in a body, led by Wuerl's band to the 12-coach Chicago and North Western train which will leave at 11:45am for Elkhart Lake. There is another special train bringing the Sturgeon Bay and Green Bay employees which will meet them at about 12:45 o'clock and the fun will begin. There will be a big program of entertainment until 8 o'clock in the evening when the trains will leave for the trip back home.

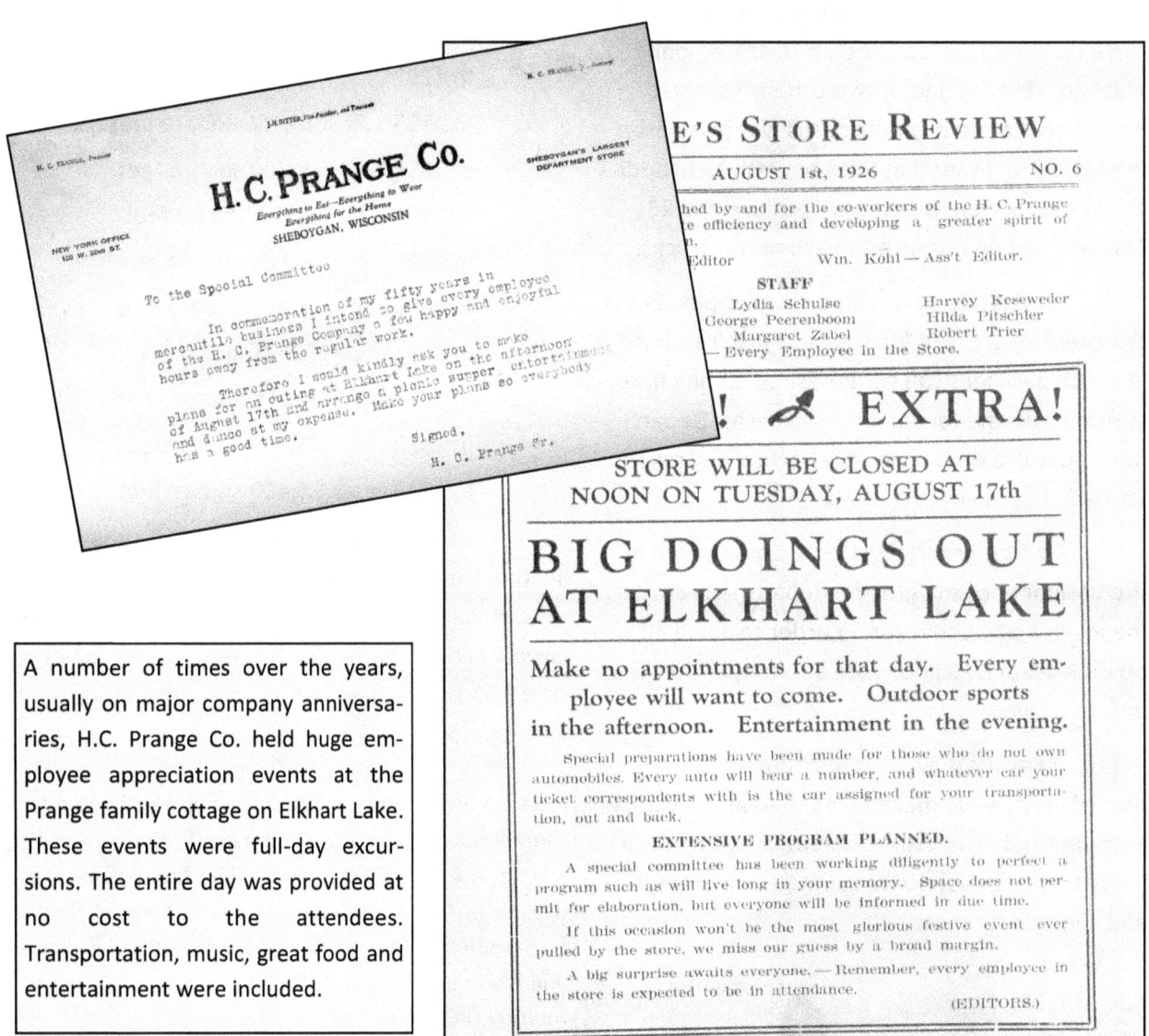

A number of times over the years, usually on major company anniversaries, H.C. Prange Co. held huge employee appreciation events at the Prange family cottage on Elkhart Lake. These events were full-day excursions. The entire day was provided at no cost to the attendees. Transportation, music, great food and entertainment were included.

AFTERNOON PROGRAM

Band Concert . . . . . Elkhart Lake Band

All games in charge of E. Hoyer, assisted by Eitel Meyer, Art. Hiltgen and Herbert Froh.

1:30 P. M.—Start of Automobile Parade.
3:00 P. M.—Indoor Baseball Game. (outside) 7 innings, 1 prize for winners.

The Wears		The Eats
Capt. E. Hoyer		Capt. Bert Sutter
C. Ruppel	First Base	B. Sutter
R. Trotter	Second Base	J. Bayens
W. Paulman	Third Base	E. Voelker
W. Bub, R. Daniels	Right Field	J. Ruppel
C. Laue, A. Grabowsky	Center Field	A. Grosskopf
J. Daniels, W. Voigt	Left Field	A. Lacselles
A. Hierseman	Right Short Stop	B. Fahre
W. Plehn	Left Short Stop	W. Ebs
C. Raatz	Pitcher	Ed. Vo
E. Hoyer	Catcher	M. Sie

Official Umpire—Arno Keppler

During the time of the Baseball game, swimming and contests will be staged under the guidance of Herbert Fr Della Draeger. Prizes for fastest swimmer and best div

4:15 P. M.—50 yard dash for girls under 125 lbs.
4:25 P. M.—50 yard dash for girls under 300 lbs.
4:35 P. M.—Bottle Filling Contest—For Couples
4:45 P. M.—Doughnut Eating Contest—For Girls
4:55 P. M.—Three Legged Race—For Men
5:05 P. M.—Balloon Blowing Contest—For Girls
5:15 P. M.—Pipe Smoking Contest—For Couples
5:25 P. M.—Pop Drinking Contest—For Everybody
5:30 P. M.—Old Fashioned Games—For Everybody
until   Forget for a little while th
dinner time   have grown up and enjoy
                     the games of your boy and

Picnic at Elkhart Lake

GIVEN TO THE EMPLOYEES OF

H. C. PRANGE COMPANY

BY

H. C. PRANGE, SR.

IN COMMEMORATION OF HIS

FIFTY YEAR SERVICE

IN THE MERCANTILE BUSINESS

August the seventeenth
nineteen hundred twenty-six

1876 PRANGE'S EMPLOYEES' PICNIC 1926

1926 Celebration items

Opposite page, Upper left, invitation from 1926 event, signed by H.C. Prange.

Opposite page, right, 1926 Prange Company Review, advertisement for celebration.

This page, left—page from 1926 event program.

This page, right— cover of 1926 event program.

Bottom, 1926 event

Many modes of transportation were used to visit Prange's over the years. These photos are interesting because they were both taken in the 1920s. The image above is dated January of 1929 and the photo below is sometime after 1927 because of the presence of the Model As. Cutters and horses were still used to deal with the snow each winter into the 1930s and 1940s. Snow tires and poor road conditions made the cutter a better choice.

Four Stories of Success
The 1930-1960s

At Prange's in Sheboygan it has always been the customer who is central, ergo the mantra, *"the customer is always right."* The slogan, *"It's not yours 'til you like it"*, was another hard and fast rule, created by H.C. Prange and put into action by Prange employees. Customer service was one foundation of the Prange business. This was seen and put into action through the constant changes that kept the store fresh and attractive to customers.

The image above is the iconic view of H.C. Prange Co. that we all know and love. But, even this view changed multiple times over the decades.

Physical expansion of the Sheboygan store increased retail space more that eighty times from the original store at Eighth and Wisconsin. Of the fifteen major expansion projects during the first seventy-five years, the most important were:

* Erection of a new four-story building on the original site in 1923. Complete remodeling and renovation of the store interior in 1937, including installation of Wisconsin's first department store escalator.
* Installation of the downstairs budget store immediately following World War Ii.
* Opening of the new auxiliary household appliance store, immediately south of the main building, in 1957.
* New fourth floor warehouse store for furniture.

The store was in a constant state of flux. New departments were added as needed like the bakery and basement sale department. Other were discontinued as they became obsolete, like the millinery department with its veiled hats and finery and the wedding mantilla head piece department.

Firsts were also important to the company. They represented cutting edge service. Prange listened to his customer and tried to meet and even anticipate their needs.

This forward-thinking business attitude also applied to employee benefits. Prange's was among the first employers to provide paid vacations and operate on a five-day, 40 hour work week. Later a sick leave policy under which regular associates were entitled to one month's net earnings for each year of service up to one full year of illness.

Prange's also had a pension and profit-sharing plan with nearly half of the company's profits going into the plan annually. Promotions almost always came from within the store.

Carl Prange Gets Preview of Exposition

New York—H. Carl Prange, president of H.C. Prange company, Sheboygan, was given a preview of the New York World's Fair 1939 today as guest of Grover A. Whalen, president of the Fair Corporation, following a luncheon in the $740,000 administration building attended by store execs from 28 cities.

Prange's Mutual Aid Society Elects Officers At Meeting

Fabian Ourada was elected president of the H.C. Prange company's Employees' Mutual Aid Society at its 27th annual meeting and banquet in Turner Hall Thursday night.

Excellent Report
. . . Following the singing of "America," the banquet was served with music provided by the Wurlitzer Accordion band, under the direction of Frederick Kuether.

In the report of the president of the society it was reported the society has paid sick claims amounting to $31,525.86 and hospital benefits to the amount of $7,531.81 showing that the organization has been of invaluable aid to its members during times of sickness.

. . After the meeting was adjourned presented the girls' octet, who sang three splendid numbers. Charles Nash and his stooge, Ralph Spears, entertained with a sleight-of-hand performance which was loudly applauded.

After the entertainment dancing was enjoyed to the music of Eddie Simms' orchestra. High spot in the dancing was two dances staged by the "Jitterbugs."

These images of H.C. Prange's new beauty parlor were taken on March 27, 1933. They are part of the Sheboygan Press collection.

Both departments are decorated in the Art Deco style popular here in the 1920s. Operators were qualified to give facials, manicures, machine and machineless permanents, hand treatments and scalp treatments. The salon also stocked a complete line of beauty preparations.

The backbone of Prange's business was the farmer. Farmers brought their produce (i.e. apples, potatoes, eggs, milk, berries) to the store and were given "due bills" in exchange.

These due bills or certificates (booklet seen at left) could be used only at Prange's and were spent like cash. This exchange system was a way for people for whom cash was scarce to buy items they needed (shoes, clothing, cooking utensils, and a few fineries). For some farmers it was a weekly stop; for others it was a highly anticipated special event. Prange's treatment of the farmer created an intense loyalty which benefitted both shopper and store.

Steve Gabrielse, above, of rural Sheboygan brought garden produce by wagon to the H.C. Prange Company for upwards of forty years. The image, taken June 24, 1932, shows Mr. Gabrielse with his horses and buggy filled with produce parked outside Prange's waiting to unload. The farmers unloaded at the Wisconsin Avenue entrance.

Prange's always had a policy to pay two cents more per dozen for eggs than any other competition would pay. Once, during an egg pricing war in the 1930s, the store bought 400 cases of eggs, thirty dozen eggs in a case (That's 144,000 eggs). The company had to ship an entire freight car load to Boston just to get rid of them.

During the national bank holiday of 1933, Prange's accepted checks from customers and issued due bills, many of which were used to pay dental or doctor bills or buy groceries. People had no money. The checks weren't cashed until the moratorium was over.

The Banking Crisis of 1933. A banking panic sparked into flame about three weeks before the inauguration of Franklin Delano Roosevelt. Like a prairie fire, it spread throughout the nation as alarmed customers rushed to their banks to empty their accounts. The panic ruined numerous banks. On the day before Roosevelt took office, more than 5,000 banks went under. The new president announced a "bank holiday" on March 6, 1933, and closed every bank in the country. They would remain closed until Department of the Treasury officials could inspect each institution's ledgers. Banks in viable financial condition would be primed with Treasury money and permitted to do business again. Those found in marginal condition were kept closed until they could be restored to a sound footing. Numerous banks that had been poorly run remained closed forever.

Wedding Scene is Attraction at Style Show

The high point in the H.C. Prange company's annual spring fashion clinic, which had 1,200 in attendance was the wedding scene pictured at left as the models showed gowns for the 1939 bride and her attendants. Miss Marie Burke, center, is wearing the bridal gown. Misses Mary Jane Walters, left and Irene Zuidmulder, right are attendants. Jewel Dean Trudell is the flower girl.

Fifteen models displayed nearly 100 garments in the spring and summer show. The garments shown confirmed this year's tendency toward femininity. The clinic was conducted by Mrs. Maude Thompson, Chicago.

THE SHEBOYGAN PRESS, WEDNESDAY, DECEMBER 6, 1933

Selection Is Easier Where Assortments Are Larger And Prices Are Usually Thriftier, Too!

It's Easy To Find The Right Gift For Every One At H.C. Prange Co.
Open Friday Evenings Until Christmas

Men Like Practical Gifts!

Fancy Shirts $1.95

Arrow Shirts Sanforized shrunk. Plain colors and fancy patterns. Collar attached. All sizes. Prices start at $1.95

Silk Neckties Silks, silk and wool, wools, satins and homespuns. Fancies makes many patterns. Prices start 48c

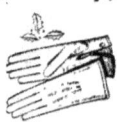
Pigtex Gloves Regulars and Cadets, sizes 7½ to 10½. Snap wrist, slip-on styles. $1.69

Smart Pajamas Made of fine quality broadcloth in beautiful patterns. V-neck, slip-over and notch collars. A, B, C, D. $1.95

Interwoven Hose Interwoven wool hose in checks and English ribs. Sizes 10½ to 12. Other wool hose 35c and 50c. $1.00

Handkerchiefs Made by Arrow. A splendid assortment of mammoth patterns. Boxed at 25c.

Suede Blazers Suede leather jackets with zipper front, two pockets and reinforced collar, cuffs and bottoms. 36 to 46. $6.50

Silk Mufflers Made of pure silk and finished with silk fringed ends. A wide range of patterns and colors. $1.95

Formal Shirts Arrow's "Kirk" Sizes 14½ to 16½. 1 or 2 studs. $3.

Slippers For Every One!

Men's Romeos Brown kid leather uppers in natural colors. Soft rubber heel. Fully lined. Well made. $1.98

Men's Everetts Brown kid uppers with leather soles and rubber heels. Well made. Smart looking. $1.39

Child's Moccasins Misses' and children's leather moccasin style slippers. Warm lining. Sizes 9 to 2. 69c

Ladies' Hylos Sheep's wool slippers in natural colors. Double chrome leather sole. Sizes 2 to 8. $1.23

Ladies' Comforts Fine quality kid leather uppers in assorted colors. Padded soles and heels. $1.19

Bunny Slippers Misses' and children's. Double chrome leather sole. Bunny boxes. Sizes 11 to 2s at 89c. 79c

Men's Genuine Leather Comfort Slippers at 89c
Main Floor

Gifts That Boys Like!

Silk Neckties Fancy hand styles in new polka dot checks and others. Prices 25c... 19c

Dress Shirts Kaynee, Mottel and Shirtcraft brands in plains and fancies. All sizes for boys and youths. Prices $1.50 to— 79c

Smart Pajamas Broadcloth pajamas in middy or coat styles with contrasting trims. One and two-piece. Prices $1.50 to— 79c

Warm Sweaters Pullover styles with V, crew or turtle neck. Plain with contrasting trims. Sizes 4 to 16. Prices $2.98 and up. 98c

Assorted Blazers Melton cloth, tweeduroy and mackinaw cloth. Button or zipper styles. Plaids and plains. Prices $2.98 to— $1.64

Dressy Scarfs Square and oblong mufflers and some in Mickey Mouse styles. Packed in fancy boxes. Prices 50c to— 59c

Boys' Shop...2nd Floor

Special Purchase! ... Mandalay Lingerie
In Time For Christmas!
De Luxe Rayons..... "Soft As a Tropical Breeze"

Vests — Built-up shoulders and bodice tops. Regular and extra sizes all at each....
Panties — Band tops with re-inforced gussets. Sizes 34 to 42. Extra sizes at 89c each....
Bloomers — Regulation style. Re-inforced gussets. Sizes 34 to 42. Extra sizes at 89c each....

79c ea. *In Fancy Gift Box!*

Chemise — Bodice top with flare bottom. Bodice top with cuff bottom. All sizes. Sizes from 34 to 42. **89c**

Beautifully tailored from the finest rayons and "soft as a tropical breeze." The kind of lingerie you would like to receive as a Christmas gift yourself... and the kind that is easy on the purse. Don't confuse Mandalay with ordinary rayon lingerie for it is far superior in every way... and very unusual at this special price. Come early tomorrow while the selection is at its best. Solve several of your gift problems with Mandalay at these special prices.
Main Floor

"Peau De Velour" Pure Silk Gowns
54 inches long. Tailored with embroidery trims or elaborately lace trimmed. Wide shoulder effects. Flesh, tea rose or blue. Reg. $3.50 **$2.94**
Second Floor

Answer many gift problems with
New Handkerchiefs

6 for 75c Men's plain linen handkerchiefs in good generous sizes. Neat hems. Fine quality.

3 for $1 Men's fine linen handkerchiefs with woven corded border and fancy initial. Large size.

6 for 75c Ladies' plain white linen handkerchiefs with spoke stitch. Fine for gift giving.

Men's Linen Initial Handkerchiefs With Narrow Hems. At 15c

Men's Linen Handkerchiefs With Woven Striped Borders. At 25c
Main Floor

The Holidays Will Require One of These

Fur Coats Look Their Best With
Metallic Hats
$2.45

Black, brown, blue, red and rust with combinations of metallic cloth in gold and silver. They give your fur coats and fur collars a touch of brightness. Smart borders.
Second Floor

New Frocks
$15

Dinner Frocks, Tavern Frocks, Afternoon Frocks, Formal Gowns

You'll never be able to go through the holidays without one or two frocks like these in your wardrobe... and you won't want to either after you see how lovely these are. Gay new shades that have a clever way of flattering... interesting new details that make you glad fashion has approved romantic elegance. Get at least one new frock for yourself.
2nd Floor

A Warm Welcome Is Assured These New
Flannel Robes
$3.98 Up To $7.50

Rose! Green! Red! Blue! Orchid!

Clever new robes for ladies and misses in styles so smart a warm welcome is assured every one of them. Shawl collars or notch collars! Patch pockets! Belts of same material! Contrasting and metal trims. Small, medium, large and extra large sizes. What a variety there is to choose from! What lovely gifts they'll make!
Second Floor...Sport Shop

Smart Gifts!
Leather Bags
$2.95

Pouch and envelope style leather bags in assorted grains and styles. All have coin purse and mirrors. Black and various shades of brown. Many clever shapes.

For Mother: Double Top Strap Bags in Black or Brown At $5.98 To $10.95
Main Floor

Every Woman Will Recognize The Superior Quality Of
No-Mend Silk Hose
$1.15 $1.35 And $1.65

Chiffon and service weight silk stockings that will not only be recognized as being of superior quality but will prove their worth with longer service than anyone would expect from such cob-webby sheerness.

Tested by the Better Fabrics Testing Bureau...And Approved
Main Floor

Here's an easy way to the hearts of Young Misses!
Smart New Dresses

- Velvets
- Taffetas
- Plain Silk
- Printed Silk
- Combinations

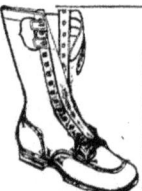
Boys' Hi-Tops Sizes 11 to 2 **$2.48** Sizes 2½ to 5½ **$2.87**

Honest-Sheboygan-Made hi-tops that will keep the boy's feet warm and dry all winter. Misses', Children's and Boys' Classmate Hi-Tops at $2.79 and $2.99.
Main Floor

3 to 6 Years $1.98 Up To $5.98

7 to 14 Years $1.98 Up To $6.98

Velvets with white crepe collars and cuffs and hand lace trims! Scotch plaid skirts with velvet jackets! Flare skirted taffetas with novelty trims! Plain and printed silks with interesting new details.

Solid color silk crepes with hand smocking! Wool crepes with perky sleeve and angora stitchings! Wool jerseys in jumper effect with cotton or silk blouses! Porcelets, broadcloths, batistes, organdies and dimities in a splendid assortment of clever styles.
Children's Shop...2nd Floor

Tea Aprons
Very Smart! **59c**

A gift that is always welcomed. Pretty printed patterns with smart ruffle trims and unbleached fabrics with bright novelty and colored bindings. Fine for gifts.

Fancy Dimity Aprons With Hand Embroidery Trims........$1.19
Silks, Woolens, Jerseys, Percales, Dimities, Batistes, Organdies
Cotton Shop—2nd Floor

H. C. PRANGE CO.
SHEBOYGAN'S LARGEST DEPARTMENT STORE

H. C. Prange Co.
..will..
CLOSE Tonight And Tuesday At 6 P.M.

and remain

OPEN Till 9 P.M. Wed., Thurs., Fri. and Sat.

H. C. PRANGE CO.
SHEBOYGAN'S LARGEST DEPARTMENT STORE

HELP!
YOU'RE NEEDED

HELP — YOU ARE NEEDED — Yes, everyone connected with the H. C. Prange Company is needed to put over the Greatest Business this year than of any previous season. Right now you can increase your sales by posting the customers on the fine arrays of new Spring and Summer things we have here for their selection. Help them with your suggestions. Show the merchandise that style has decreed fitting for Spring and Summer. With the season being considerably backward, we must crowd all the business we can into the next few months — so help — CO-WORKERS — Each and every one of you get our share of the Spring and Summer Business. Swell your sales all you can.

The Cost of Worthwhile Success is "Work"

1930s Christmas time advertising for the H.C. Prange Company — holiday sales, holiday help wanted and holiday specials.

Sheboygan Press
March 25, 1936
New Basement Store To Have A Big Opening
H.C. Prange Co. Will Stage Celebration For Fifteen Departments With Complete Lines

A new Basement Store with complete lines of popular priced merchandise lavishly displayed in fifteen new departments, equal to any that can be found anywhere in the state of Wisconsin, will be opened by the H.C. Prange Company with a grand celebration beginning Thursday and continuing through Monday. It is another step in the progressive policy established several years ago by the founders of this institution.

Since this is to be one of the greatest "parties" in the history of the big department store, detailed arrangements are being made to handle the enormous crowds that are expected. Carnations will be presented to all the women visitors in the new Basement Store on Thursday and free balloons will delight the hearts of the youngsters.

Carrying as its slogan *"The Economy Spot of All Sheboygan,"* Prange's new bargain basement will inaugurate a new era in the history of the company. There will be fifteen new departments with almost every conceivable type of merchandise. The entire basement has been modernized and rearranged to accommodate them.

Bright and Cheerful
The new Basement Store will be a cheerful place to shop. It will be one of the most modern, best lighted stores in the city. The merchandise will be displayed on modern, open-top glass bin tables and on the newest display racks. The same fashion requirements will apply for the Basement Store that have always given distinction to the upstairs store. The same buyers will select the merchandise for both stores. The Prange reputation will be back of every article. The same services, such as charge accounts, letters of credit and free accounts, and free delivery will apply, with prompt and courteous attention to every one.

In a gay color scheme of green and ivory, the new Basement Store will be a delight to every shopper. The space occupied by the fifteen bargain departments is so large that a vast display of merchandise is possible, with an almost limitless choice of materials, sizes, colors and styles.

Open-Top Tables
The new open-top tables make it possible to arrange the merchandise by sizes so that it may be conveniently selected by the shopper. All of the goods are within reach of the customer and can be easily inspected. In the women's dress, coat and suit department there are new display racks, three-way mirrors and a large number of fitting rooms for prompt service.

The new departments that will form the basement store are as follows: blankets, bedding and domestics; men's furnishings and apparel; boys' furnishings, cotton dresses and smocks; women's and children's hosiery; women's and children's lingerie; infants' and children's wear; millinery; five big popular dress sections; five big popular dress sections; large coat and suit section; small rugs and curtains; paper novelties; sporting goods; toys and bicycles.

Completely Modernized

While the new basement store was being constructed, the remainder of the basement, devoted to hardware and housewares, paints and wallpaper and automotive departments, was also modernized and now presents an appearance and arrangement with new fixtures and an easily accessible display of merchandise greeting the shopper. A postal substation and mail order departments will remain in the basement as heretofore. It is expected that the four-day opening celebration beginning this community, drawing thousands of people from the extensive Sheboygan trading area.

Will Cut Huge Cheese Thursday
Sheboygan Press
November 11, 1936

In the picture at right is Miss Lydia Best with the huge one-ton cheese now on display in the H.C. Prange company grocery on Thursday. John H. Peters, Plymouth, veteran cheese maker, supervised the making of the cheese, and he was assisted by Ernest Tracy, Edwin Conger, Edwin Schroeder, Arno Sass, Fred Kruschke and State Inspector Ad. Valesky. More than nine tons of milk were used in making the cheese.

H.C. Prange was a major distributor of cheese, mailing or shipping cheese to all fifty states from the Sheboygan store. This was one of the services which started soon after the original store was in business. By 1939 the cheese department featured 131 types of loaf or packaged cheese. Tourists and traveling salesmen began the practice of sending cheese to their friends for gifts.   Special promotions, like the giant cheese, kept the cheese business interesting and in the news.

Personal Shoppers Will Take Care Of Orders
February 2, 1937
Modern Switchboard Will Furnish Personal Service To Shoppers At Prange's Store

A new and modern switchboard, the third of its kind to be installed in the state, gives Sheboygan shoppers immediate contact with specially trained personal-shoppers at the H.C. Prange company store here. The other two switchboards similar to this one have been installed in large department stores at Milwaukee recently. With this new service, boasting of ten trunk lines, the shopper needs but to sit at his or her telephone, call 5600 and a lady, under the supervision of Marie Freimuth, will do the shopping as directed. This personal shopper knows the prices of articles and the different grades available. She can answer all your questions and immediately turn over your order to the proper department, according to C.A. Windness, advertising manager for the company.

Delays Eliminated
Delays are eliminated since there are from six to eight girls working constantly at the long switchboard. There are no stops nor waits between your call and the placing of your order. Instead of being transferred from department to department as you put in your order, your complete inquiry is centralized with one person who takes your order and your instructions.

Shown above is the new "express" switchboard which has recently been installed in the H.C. Prange company store. The girls seated at the board are personal shoppers who take your order and refer it to other departments through the aid of messengers. In the back row, seated, from left to right, are Marie Holtz, Caroline Kent, Marie Freimuth, supervisor, and Velva Schwaller. Front row, from left to right are Constance Jesinski, Madeline Theis, Charlotte Farchman and Ella Oehnke.

Business calls will still be handled over 10 trunk lines running to the old switch board. The girls who handle the switch board have been trained to know the articles kept in most departments. They have first hand information concerning practically everything sold by the company. In case the shopper wishes to be connected with the department instead of talking to the personal-shopper this can be done by the personal shopper without a moment's delay. This modernized Prange service, known as the express telephone order service, should do a great deal in speeding up the entire workings of the company.

Wisconsin's Only Escalator

The summer of 1937 witnessed the opening of Prange's new escalator . . . The only moving stairway, as it was called at the time, in Wisconsin. Prange's escalator preceded those in Milwaukee by five years. The escalator took shoppers from the first floor to the second floor, but not back down.

The escalator was electrically driven, running continuously and silently, and was capable of carrying as many as 6,000 people per hour. Situated at the rear of the store the escalator ran from the first to second floors and could accommodate as many as 42 people at one time.

Escalator Background—The earliest working type of escalator, patented in 1892 by Jesse W. Reno, was introduced as a new novelty ride at the Old Iron Pier at Coney Island NY, in 1896. But, it took the Otis Elevator Company of New York to manufacture it and get it ready for general use. It was exhibited in 1900 at the Paris Exposition, where the name "escalator" was adopted.

The escalators were upgraded in 1947 when shoppers could go from the second to the third floor and also take the escalators down, as well. The originals only went up.

Among other improvements made in 1937 was the installation of an up-to-date soda fountain and luncheon service. This new department on the main floor offered the latest in comfort and convenience for customers. Tables were Formica-topped steel tables and had comfortable genuine red leather and chrome chairs. The table tops were advertised as scorch and scratch-proof. The tables also had purse and package rails for the comfort of the customers. Ninety people could be seated at one time.

Improvements were constantly being made at Prange's as the need for them arose. As a result the store enjoyed the reputation of being one of the finest and most complete stores in Wisconsin. Prange's placed customer confidence first among all its assets.

H. C. Prange Toy Prices

Each of the following toys sold for just 47 cents during the Christmas season of 1937.
Ping Pong Sets; Baseball Dart games; Miscellaneous Dolls; Wonderscope Micro Sets; Mickey and Minnie Mouse Tea Sets; Sets of Doll House furniture; Regular Feller's Football Pants; Pioneer Builder Log Cabin Set ; Doll Lawn Swings; Cross Country Ring Games; Betty Boop Toy Tea Sets; Little Orphan Annie Tea Sets.

Prange's Golden Jubilee Year was 1937– Fifty years of service. Evidence of the celebration seen here as the store was decorated with a large cake– corner of Eighth Street and Wisconsin Avenue.

Golden Jubilee Celebration

More than 1,000 employees and spouses invaded Elkhart Lake on July 13, 1937 in order to celebrate Prange's Golden Jubilee of the store's founding. Employees came by train from Green Bay, Sturgeon Bay and Sheboygan. Two special trains brought friends to Elkhart Lake, arriving about 12:45p.m. They were met by members of the Wuerl Band playing marching music. The delegation swung south from the depot to Siebken's, Schwartz's, Osthoff's and the Pine Point hotels, all of which had been taken over by the company for the day. One of the features of the parade was the clown band made up of employees of the Green Bay store.

The day included scenic boat rides on Elkhart Lake, swimming, dancing at the Schwartz Hotel, athletic events and competition, a special bratwurst luncheon at Fireman's Park and finally a talent show at the Pine Point Hotel.

Prange's Carpet and Drapery Department— Behind the selling floor are the behind the scenes workrooms. This is where the made-to-order items are crafted, whether it's carpeting, seen below circa 1939, or slip-covers or draperies. Experienced workmen crafted items with flawless tailoring and workmanship. Fluorescent lighting was a new and innovative addition to the department in the 1940s. It was described as being easier on the eyes and it enabled the buyer to see what it would look like in their own home.

Dollar Days
1940s

H.C Prange Dollar Days Celebration

Downtown Sheboygan was crowded as thousands of Sheboygan shoppers surged into the store to snap up values they had seen advertised. The rush continued throughout the entire day. No merchandise was spared. Men's shirts and hosiery were usually the busiest counters of the day.

Girls' Clothing 1940s

Notions and Art Department 1940s

Home Décor and Fine Furnishing Departments

Above, Prange's shoe department, 1942. Prange's shoe sections were known for quality, style and service. Besides dress shoes, Prange's carried a complete line of nurses' oxfords, men's heavy duty work shoes, rubbers and galoshes. Each pair was scientifically fitted by X-ray to insure perfect fit and lasting comfort. Prange also had a shoe repairman (cobbler) in house to repair shoes.
Below, Women's Coats and Ready to Wear, 1942. Advertised as Fashion With Economy.

Moving Picture On Fishing Being Shown at Store

A one-hour, two-reel motion picture of one of the world's greatest sports, tuna fishing, is being shown in the grocery of the H.C. Prange company today and Saturday. The picture, parts of which are in beautiful natural color, has for its setting Terminal Island, California.

Terminal Island is the headquarters for fishermen and its located near San Francisco. The entire story of the tuna fish is told, from the time the boats go out into the Pacific until the time the fish they catch are packed and shipped. Of great interest is the scenery of the West coast.

Showing the picture is Mr. Murray, representative of the Van Camp company. A tuna fish is cut and on display in the grocery. The hours when the motion picture will be shown are: 4:30, 6:30 and 8p.m. today. Tomorrow the picture will be shown at 1:30, 3 and 4:30p.m.

Prange's Carry Five Complete Pattern Service

McCall, Hollywood, Simplicity, Butterick and Vogue patterns are carried.

H.C. Prange Company Store Is A Community Institution

Sheboygan Press
July 31, 1942

Prange's—a metropolitan store in a medium-sized city—more than a mere store, an institution with character and reputation embedded in the community—an enterprise that has grown with Sheboygan for 55 years. When the late H.C. Prange founded this great department store in 1887, Sheboygan had 15,000 people. The city and the store have grown up together. Prange's has advertised the name of Sheboygan far and wide throughout the country.

The business was incorporated in 1898 under the name of H.C. Prange company. Along with sales volume, the store's physical plant grew rapidly. The present large store was built and opened in 1923. The H.C. Prange company acquired its store in Green Bay in 1927 and the Sturgeon Bay store in 1930. In its three stores the Prange company employs 576 full-time regular employees, besides many extra employees.

From time to time the Sheboygan store has been renovated and remodeled to keep pace with its increasing sales volume. The present modernization program, now in its seventh year, started in 1936. The escalator—that saver of tired legs with almost limitless capacity—is one of the few in this part of the country. Five years old, it was the first installed in any Wisconsin department.

Handsome Store Front
This summer many comments have been heard from tourists about Prange's handsome store front. The citizens of the community are already proud of it, but to hear praise from outsiders who have perhaps seen stores in larger cities makes it doubly sure that the Prange company has as attractive a store front as any in the Midwest.

Probably the prize attraction at Prange's, to which hundreds of women are drawn every season, is the Wishmaker House. In this lovely model home the bride's dreams of her ideal house are realized. Here the homemaker can furnish her place along one consistent pattern. She can choose a particular design or color she likes best and then fit every article in her home to that design or color—from glassware to beds.

Reservoir of Ideas
Ideas for the beautification of the home are born in the Wishmaker House. A housewife may see some color or design that gives her an idea that brings about a pleasant change in her household setup. The Prange Company is one of the two representatives of the Wishmaker House in Wisconsin.

The apparel departments for women and children are stocked with all the delightful and exclusive styles that make American women the best dressed in the world. The piece goods department on the second floor is a panorama of everything in yard goods the modern woman can desire.

Buyers Go East

To satisfy its patrons' demands for the latest in style merchandise, the Prange company regularly sends its buyers to the New York market to study the newest fashion trends and keep stocks fresh. A regional buying office is maintained in New York to augment the buyers' efforts and keep them steadily informed of up-to-the-minute events in the fashion capital.

On the street floor is the men's wear department. The newest styles and colors in the latest men's wearables are available in this section of the store, which does a very large volume of business. Also on the main floor is the shoe department, one of the largest in the state, carrying an amazingly large stock. For men the Freeman shoe is featured, while there is the Rice-O'Neill Fashion shoes for the ladies. This department is even able to supply orders for Dutch wooden shoes.

The grocery department, of course, has received statewide patronage. Outside people who visit Prange's marvel at the size and extent of this department where everything in foods can be purchased. The store was the first in the state to suggest cheese packages as Christmas gifts and appeared in the *House and Garden* magazine.

Requests for shipments of this unique Christmas gifts poured in from all parts of the nation. In fact, Prange's received orders from 46 of the 48 states, besides Bermuda, Hawaii and Central America. The Christmas gift package consisted of seven varieties of natural cheese in colorful Yuletide wrapping.

Another service rendered the community is the postal station in the basement. Great piles of mail are happily sent from this office every day. The station also writes money orders, sells stamps, handles parcels, and performs other postal duties.

The mark of the outstanding department store is its attention to the welfare of its employees. In the Prange company there is the Employees' Aid Society, which provides sickness and hospital benefits for the employees. The company and employees share in contributing to this fund. Prange's also has a retirement fund for long-service employees. This fund is contributed solely by the H.C. Prange company.

New Paved Parking Lot—1944

Designed for the automobile – navigated shopper, a paved parking area for 25 automobiles was constructed east of the grocery department with easy accessibility to the building. Parking time was limited to one hour. The lot was monitored by an attendant.

From the *Milwaukee Journal*—Date unknown— To this day, many directions for locations in Sheboygan are given in relation to an old landmark, the Prange store. Mrs. Olivia Laatch recently told the Gordon Heckers of Oostburg that the store really was the geographical hub of the city back in the 1930s when her husband, Larry, was transferred by the Wisconsin Telephone Co. from Milwaukee to Sheboygan. She remembered Larry asking a Sheboyganite where the telephone company office was. "Just go up the street to Prange's," the old settler told him, "then come back one block."

New Escalators At Prange's Store Are In Operation Now

Sheboygan Press

July 1, 1947

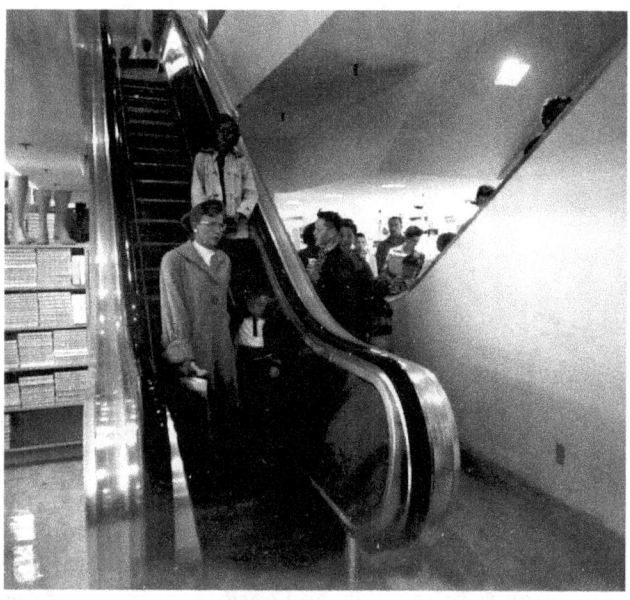

With a minimum of fanfare the new escalators at the H.C. Prange company store here went into operation this morning, and early shoppers officially christened the escalators by riding up to the second floor, up to the third, and back down again. It was the first time in many months that escalator service was available. It was the first time shoppers could take the escalator up to the third floor. And it was the first time that a shopper could take the escalators down as well as up. But there was another "first" that preceded these. The old escalator at the store that carried shoppers from the main floor to the second floor was the first escalator to be installed in any department store in Wisconsin. Built in 1937, it preceded the installation of escalators in Milwaukee department stores by five years. The new escalators are of modernistic design and have safety tread steps, flexible composition handrails, side panels of stainless steel, and stainless steel brim. Custom-built for the H.C. Prange company, they have all the improvements of modern engineering. Absolutely foolproof, they have every safety features. Smooth and silent in operation, they require less power than elevators. Company officials pointed out today the advantages in convenience to the customer. The capacity of the escalators is such that peak crowds can be handled with ease and without crowding, and the period of waiting that handicaps shoppers using elevators is eliminated entirely. Capacity of the escalators is about 6,000 persons an hour. Elevator service at the store will be continued, however, partly to provide service to the basement and fourth floor, partly to serve persons who have baby buggies or bulky parcels to take from one floor to another and partly to serve those who prefer elevators.

Sprinkler System Prevents Prange Store Conflagration

Only the store's automatic sprinkler system prevented a fire of undetermined origin from becoming a major conflagration at the H.C. Prange company store at 4:30 this morning. The fire, which started in the men's locker room in the basement, was discovered by one of the night men just as the flames were licking the sides and top of one of the wooden lockers. A pail of water was immediately dashed onto the flame, but did little toward putting out the flame, which continued until enough heat was generated to set off four of the automatic sprinklers in the locker room. When the alarm was turned in the entire fire department responded, but little work remained for them to do, other than open windows and get rid of the water. . . . Officials of the company estimated the damages not to exceed $200.

H.C. Prange Co. used every means possible to enable customers to carefully and easily buy items for everyday living. Always finding new ways to serve its customers, Prange's was one of the first stores to have its own charge card, lay-away plan and letters of credit. These items were modern extensions of the popular due bill program.

Hundreds Use Letters of Credit to Solve Family Buying Problems

A letter of credit is as good as cash for purchases made in every department except the grocery. The cashier deducts the amount of each purchase from the letter itself, thereby giving the purchaser a record of the amount of credit used and the amount remaining to be used. H.C. Prange Co. issues 90-day Letters of Credit without carrying charge. Where the period of payments covers a longer period, only a small charge is added.

Charga-Plate System
To Be Installed in Prange Store

The H.C. Prange company will soon revolutionize the handling of its charge sales with the introduction of the Charga-Plate system, exclusive to its stores in Sheboygan, Green Bay and Sturgeon Bay.

The Charga-Plate is a small embossed metal plate which charge customers carry for identification. This plate, when placed in the addresser actually prints all the needed information on the sales receipt.

The main features of the Charga-Plate system are the saving of the customer's time in shopping and the elimination of the need to having customers repeat or spell their names or addresses.

Prange's Washburn and Sturgeon Bay also used the Charga-Plate. Sturgeon Bay was the smallest city in the United States to use this type of credit card. Another first of its kind—the Prange card could be used in any of the three Prange's stores.

Lay-Away Plan Proved Convenient Buying Method

Another of H.C. Prange's solutions to the ever present "short on cash" dilemma for its customers was its Lay-Away plan. The customer was required to put just a small percentage down on each item and then was responsible for a regular monthly payment. There was no interest charge. When the item was paid in full it was able to be picked up.

Editorial Note from *The Press*

No Truth To Rumor

For the past three or four months there has been a rumor in Sheboygan that the H.C. Prange Co. has sold or was about to sell its store in this city. These rumors continued to grow until it became a part of the daily routine of conversation.

Today we are privileged to announce that we have run to the ground these rumors and can state for an absolute fact that there is no foundation to any of them. The H.C. Prange Co. has never offered its store for sale, neither has it any intentions of selling.

A war period always breeds rumor, hysteria, and emotional instability. Charley Broughton, the editor of *The Sheboygan Press*, adopted a novel method to stop a rumor that was prevalent in Sheboygan. The rumor centered in the story that the H.C. Prange company, the largest store in Sheboygan, was about to sell. The Press assured the Sheboygan community that there was nothing to the yarn in a front page statement—The (Madison) Capital Times.

A preview of styles for spring were shown at the H. C. Prange company "Victory" Fashion Parade in the department store. Those who modeled are seen above (left to right) Jean Fay, Eugenie Keltam, Josephine O'Brien, Betty Eichwald, Mary Jane Walters, Pearl Hujet, Connie Gott, Maralyn Quintal, Genevieve Indra. Youngsters are (left to right) June Raymaker, Tommy Huxford and Judy Garot.

Silver Edge Bakery

Images of the Silver Edge Bakery from the 1940s. The images on the left and above show the bright and airy preparation areas of the bakery.

Image on the opposite page shows one of the beautiful showcases in the Bakery Department.

In October of 1942 Prange's opened its own Silver Edge Bakery. With huge rotary ovens, high speed mixers and the latest in all baking equipment. The bakery was originally located in a well-ventilated building of its own. It was later moved to an underground location, beneath the parking lot on the corner of New York Avenue and Seventh Street.

By the 1960s the staff included a bakery superintendent plus six full-time bakers and about ten other full and part-time employees working in the shop. Bakery was produced six days a week. Prange's boasted the use of the freshest ingredients, including fresh eggs and creamery butter.

The Sheboygan store was the only Prange store with a bakery. A 1960s era brochure touted many innovative pieces of equipment. They included a bread slicer which sliced an entire loaf of bread in one cutting operation. More than forty types of bread were baked each week amounting to many thousands of loaves. The bakery had two ovens that had shelves which rotated like a ferris wheel which could bake 252 loaves of bread at one time. The doughnut fryer created many treats which were served in the Fountain and Terrace Room restaurants. The giant pan washer held eighteen pans at one time which were scrubbed clean in just eleven minutes. Other specialty machines included a rack washer, cake mixers, vertical mixers, proofers, divider and bun machine, hard roll creasing machine, a steam kettle, a doughnut and éclair filler and multiple cake decorating tools. All items made here were also sold in the bakery sales area of the store.

Wishmaker's House

Furniture Department

H.C. Prange's furniture department offered furniture of superior workmanship and great style, but at moderately low prices. Many famous name manufacturers were featured including local concerns - American Chair Company, Madewell Chair, Midwest Furniture, Northern Furniture, Phoenix Chair, Sheboygan Bedding, Sheboygan Chair, Sheboygan Fibre Furniture and the Westfield Company. Prange used local producers when possible, believing that local manufacturers recognized the needs of the area and created products that met those needs.

The images on these pages document the Wishmaker's House. These ensembles were considered the finest contributions to home decorating each year. A limited number of stores in the United States were chosen to exhibit the Wishmaker's House—just two in the entire state of Wisconsin— and Prange's was selected.

Homemakers could walk through the exhibit and choose anything from one piece to the entire exhibit, knowing that the colors and styles would coordinate and transfer easily into their own homes.

Prange's also had many other model display rooms available to shoppers. A full staff of interior decorators worked in the store. They were available at no charge to the customer. New table settings were very often designed by the members of the Sheboygan Garden Club, the Business and Professional Women's Club and the Sheboygan Women's Club.

Men's Clothing

Girls' Clothing

Top: Women's Lingerie
Below: Yard Goods

Personal Buying Service Permits Shopping By Mail

Prange's inaugurated their personal shopping service about 1932. Mary Miles, the original personal shopper, handled inquiries and orders from thousands of people from almost every state in the Union.

Direct requests for specific merchandise are filled or samples for fabrics are sent. The order is sent by return mail with the postage prepaid within a radius of 150 miles. Mary also filled requests for wedding or birthday gifts with the buyer specifying price and leaving the selection to the personal shopper.

Orders placed in the morning were ready by evening for pick-up or shipping.

Kitchen Utensils and Cookware

Tools and Hardware

Men's Shirts

Women's Dresses

Huge Crowd Attends "Hatching" of Easter Egg   **March 5, 1948**

Picture standing on the raised platform at the H.C. Prange Co. store on Wisconsin Avenue is the Easter bunny which just a few moments before had hatched from the huge egg seen in the background. With the bunny are Percy Rademacher, favorite clown of Sheboygan children and Hal O'Halloran of WHBL.

Biggest Traffic Jam in History of Sheboygan

Several thousand youngsters gathered on Wisconsin Avenue between Eleventh and Eighth Streets Thursday afternoon to watch the Easter bunny pop out of the huge Easter egg, which had been suspended at the second floor level of the H.C. Prange Company for the past several weeks.

The bunny hatched out of the 12 by 18 foot egg promptly at 4:15p.m. The huge egg was lowered to a platform by a block and tackle and shortly afterward the shell of the egg broke open and out came a large yellow and white Easter bunny.

Percy Rademacher, the children's favorite clown, was on hand to present the bunny with a bunch of carrots and other gifts, and then the bunny was paraded down Eighth Street in an open car so that all the children could view it. . . . The traffic congestion was terrific. Extra police officers were assigned to handle the huge crowd and for some time after the "hatching" the vehicular traffic jammed the streets. Extra buses were put in use to handle the homeward-bound youngsters.

Terrace Room
H.C. Prange

Every Thursday the Terrace Room's menu included Sauerbraten, potato dumplings, and red cabbage.

Fridays' menu included potato pancakes.

Prange's Terrace Room (1960)

Prange's Terrace Room, a place for finer dining, is one of the most popular places to eat in Sheboygan, specializing in a quiet, relaxing atmosphere and good, home-cooked food at reasonable prices. All foods are prepared in our own clean stainless steel kitchen, from foods carefully selected from our grocery warehouse. Dinners and lunches are served from 11 a.m. to 2 p.m. and coffee and snacks are served until 4 p.m. On days when the store is open until 9 p.m. the Terrace Room is open until 7 p.m. Food from the delicatessen is prepared in this kitchen also.

Shoreroom Restaurant (1958)

While smorgasbord style dinners are hardly uncommon in Sheboygan, the smorgasbord luncheon featured each noon in Prange's delightful Shoreroom restaurant affords a welcomed change for those not desiring a heavy mid-day meal.

In this type luncheon Prange's features a variety of appetizers, salads and condiments to go with two tasty entrees. The latter changes daily, thus providing a variety for those dining out regularly.

Prange's air conditioned Shoreroom offers a pleasant opportunity for a noon break from shopping, as well as an excellent place for dinner.

Each afternoon, from 2 to 5, little snacks and coffee are available in the Shoreroom, while tea is served without charge.

In addition to the smorgasbord noon luncheon, the Shoreroom also features a variety of other moderately priced luncheons, salads, sandwiches and other snacks.

The Shoreroom derives its name from the hand painted, full color mural of the Sheboygan shoreline that decorates the room's east and south walls.

Prange's is proud, too, of its kitchen serving the Shoreroom. It is completely equipped with stainless steel counters and utensils, while all dishes are washed in a bath of steam to insure absolute cleanliness.

The store's Shoreroom, located in the basement, is operated in addition to its popular and spacious street floor restaurant, the Terrace Room.

The Postal Service

Prange's operated a complete post office in the Basement Store. All of the services of the main branch were offered there. Every type of letter or package could be sent from this department. In addition to its regular postal duties, this department wrapped and mailed gifts and customer purchases. Over 17,000 items were wrapped here for mailing each year.

You're always welcome at *Prange's* . . .

Whether it's to sign yearbooks, eat lunch or just browse, you are invited to make Prange's your headquarters. Our doors are always open to you . . . to make Prange's a part of your life.

Prange's

Upper and Lower images—Senior yearbook signing at H.C. Prange's, June, 1956.

Each year in June, hundreds of students from both Central and North High Schools would invade Prange's for one afternoon to sign yearbooks. The counters would be cleaned off and the area at the bottom of the escalator would be cleared so students could sit on the floor and check out the new yearbooks.

Senior yearbook signing at H.C. Prange Co., June, 1956

Floor Walkers
During the 1950s there was a position in the store called a Floor Walker. Floor Walkers were people who directed shoppers to the appropriate department and helped them find the items they were looking for. They had coded rings to summon them to a telephone.

Cotton Style Showings Are Held Tuesday

Two groups of spectators Tuesday learned about cottons as winter fabrics as well as for the summer season, about miracle fabrics of today and about the accessories that make the costume.

Kay Windsor's Wonderland of Cottons was featured at style shows held on the second floor of the H. C. Prange Co. Five models showed the line to advantage. Besides the regular models from the store, Kay Kendall and Andrea Lord, professional models and actresses, donned the dresses, hats and accessories. The latter two with the commentator, Beverly Bruce, who is primarily in TV and picture work, are on an eastern and midwest tour of 13 cities in which they are taking part in 40 shows.

Miss Lord is a Wisconsinite, Kansasville being the place from which she comes. She is also a singer.

Fabrics designed by Miss Grace Norman, who usually includes lovely flowers in what she originates, was in Europe last summer and the influence of the continent was seen in some of the styles, i.e., the dress inspired by stained glass in cathedral windows and another with Riviera colors.

The commentator advised that women would be individuals, that they pick up color in the fabrics and designs and emphasize it with accessories, thusly also picking up their own personalities. "Make yourself sparkle this year, try colors you never before would have dared to try, either in fabrics or accessories," she said.

Especially appealing were crease-resistant, crinkle and miracle fabrics, the latter, one that does not have to be sprinkled, merely pressed, and looks like silkalene—a mixture of cotton and nylon. Petticoats definitely are an important part of spring and summer silhouettes. Simplicity of line in dresses, which had full skirts, some having been fashioned in shirtwaist style, were fashion points. There were a number without sleeves, some with short ones, others with three-quarter length, push-up ones. Pin-tucks, pocket and button treatment were styling details.

Prange's Plan New Branch At Appleton

June 28, 1945—Plans were announced for the construction of another branch of Prange's Department Store in Appleton, Wisconsin. The property is on College Avenue in the heart of downtown Appleton.

Homemakers To Attend Meeting At Prange Store

Homemakers will come from all parts of the county to attend a meeting where H.R. Smith, manager of the grocery department, in cooperation with Miss Mary Brady, extension nutritionist at University of Wisconsin and Leona Kilborn, county home agent will use exhibits and discussion to familiarize the women with value in groceries. This meeting is the first of its kind.

Oostburg Beats Prange's 29-26

The H.C. Prange cagers lost to the Oostburg quint 29-26. A capacity crowd witnessed the game at Oostburg.

Prange League Bowlers Enjoy Banquet Monday

A banquet fit for a king, served in Charlie Pfrang's inimitable style, proved a fitting finale to the 1939-40 bowling season at Lauer's Crystal Lake tavern. Bill Hessler won honors in cracker eating.

Foods Classes Dine At Local Restaurants
By Pat Braun

Miss Joyce Ellingson's cooking I classes are completing this year's cooking experience by dining out at various restaurants.

On Tuesday, May 15, the period I class ate at the Shore Room at Prange's, where they had a choice of many menus. The sixth period class dined at the Sky Gardens last Wednesday.

Theft Of $366 Worth Of Goods Reported Here

A theft of $366 worth of men's robes and dress scarves from a shipment of merchandise from London, England to the H. C. Prange Co. was discovered late Thursday afternoon when crates from the shipment were opened at the store.

C. J. Fredrickson, special agent for the Chicago and North Western railway, called into the case, said that nine pry marks were found on the case, opening one compete side. The crate was apparently repaired very carefully so as to appear that no entry had been made.

Because of the fact that the same type nails were used to close the crate again, he believed the robbery more than likely took place at the original point of shipment in London. The shipment was handled by the railroad from Montreal, Canada, to Sheboygan.

Prange's Teen Club and Teen Board

The Sheboygan Press Friday, August 23, 1963

Teens looked at Fall Fashion Thursday in the style show at South High School auditorium where hundreds studied the ensembles modeled by local teenagers. Among the participants was this quintet, including (left to right) Miss Kay Corinth, merchandise editor of *Seventeen* and the commentator last evening; Kathy Krier, in one of the scarf-topped casual coats; Sandy Hubert, in the "cover girl" checked outfit; Kathy Maersch, in a new shift style, and Miss Jeannine, fashion coordinator for the show's sponsors. (Clair Kilton photo)

1963 Teen Board Members

Kathy May
Valeta Johnson
Jeannine Wanezek
Kathy Haaker
Rita O'Donnell
Kris Jacobson
Carol Imig
Sandra Flentje
Connie Babitz
Cathy Maersch

Info courtesy of Sandy Hubert Zagozen

Well-Staged Show Enjoyed...

Teen-Age Fashion Show Forecasts Colorful Season On The Horizon

By SHIRLEY JARVIS
Press Staff Writer

What ever happened to the sloppy teen-ager?

She certainly wasn't in evidence in last evening's stunning H. C. Prange Co. fashion show for teen-agers, staged with definite Broadway overtones at South High School.

Those who planned Thursday evening's revue didn't spare the horses! Colorful settings, carefully selected music and well-plotted themes kept the pace lively in this pioneer venture.

And there was the added fillip of having a gracious and well-informed commentator come from the big-city world of fashion to preside. Miss Kay Corinth of the Seventeen Magazine staff filled the role smoothly.

There was more than fashion in the two-hour extravaganza — the evening was wisely divided by intermission entertainment provided by that magnetic vocal-instrumental combination — the Decappa Five. The captivating folk-singers delighted their large audience with sparkling ensemble and solo selections.

Chris Schommer scored with her solo, "Summertime," by Gershwin, her appealing voice backed by an unusual rhythm pattern. Others in the exciting ensemble are Ron Klusmeier, Michael Pungercar, Joel Grollmus and John Ott.

Teen-Agers Model

Throughout a colorful evening, sharp, young models, obviously well-schooled in their assignments, trotted out an amazing array of teen fashions—from gay casuals of the slumber party and the football game to smart, dress-up ensembles that made eyes pop.

Six imaginative scenes were planned for the show—"Step to School in Style;" "Classy Cuts for the Classroom;" "Sippin' Sodas;" "Flip Fashions for Football;" "Holsome Harmony for a Hollerin' Hootenanny" and "Driftin' in Dreamland." Between scenes, Teen Board members talked informally with the commentator on fashion in general.

Each scene had its own colorful backdrop, its own properties and music.

In the going-to-school sequence, spotlight wavering from the rich plaids to the dependable camels. Pile linings of all colors—some printed in fur imitations—were in evidence.

Next, the teen-age charmers were found in the classroom, with the ever-popular sweaters and skirts taking precedence.

Layered Look

Here the audience had its first experience with the "layered look," evidently marked for emphasis this fall. Turtle-neck sweaters and dickeys were frequent additions; then came the long-sleeved shirt, possibly a suspender skirt and over every lottes. Golds, greens, soft "mailard" blue, brilliant red — all colors seem to be on the scene.

Make-believe fur sparked the offerings, with leopard at the top of the list followed closely by pony in brown-beige and black and white combinations. It appeared in weskits over straight skirts, in car coats and in toppers of all description worn over the stretch pants.

Boots In Evidence

Furry hats were seen time after time, the enticing confections in many colors and silhouettes topping all but the most sophisticated outfits. The teen-agers also modeled a wide variety of boots, ranging from ankle-height to just-below-the-knees. "No color" green was seen most often, but they were stunning in blacks and browns, and practical as all-weather attire, according to Miss Corinth.

At the "football game," the new suede cloth was observed in the toppers and here, again, pile linings scored. Scarf collars and hoods were warm features and the banner-waving models looked ready for all comers.

In the "hootenanny" interlude, a pair of red corduroy knickers raised eyebrows and the kilt skirt made its debut.

A spirited pillow fight opened the "slumber party" scene, with the "battlers" all in bright red night shirts. When they finally settled down to sleep, they had wild dreams, of course. And, of course, they dreamt of fashions—this time the stunning outfits they might wear for a stroll down New York's Fifth Avenue.

"Dream" Designs

In this exciting interlude, the audience saw an impressive black double-knit coat-jumper with pongee sheath, followed by a stunning blue wool suit dripping with fox collar and cuffs. A white coat with jaguar accents drew murmurs, along with the practical three-piece camel wool coat-jacket and skirt.

Fox appeared again on the sleeves of a menswear grey double-knit ensemble.

For after-five occasions, the young women showed inky black velvet in a graceful design; several styles featuring filmy chiffon in panels and long, full sleeves; a long evening dress of black crepe sparkling with net beads and a cape-collared number with interesting banded detail. A holiday-mood white brocade suit with fur trim drew more murmurs in this sophisticated collection.

Ski attire, also suitable for leisure hour wear, concluded the show with imports (Danish and Italian) stealing the thunder. These all topped the inevitable stretch pants and boots.

Teen Board members, who were heard during the evening, are Kathy May, Valeta Johnson, Jeannine Wanezek, Kathy Haak ordinator for H. C. Prange Co., opened the show and generally supervised the well-contrived revue, along with Ed Nagourney, division merchandise manager.

Models, in addition to the Board, were the following Teen Club members: Kris Koehn, Linda Nettekoven, Nancy Weber, Marge Schneider, Karen Kuelthau, Margaret Brickner, Jackie O'Grady, June Kisolek, Debbie Church, Linda Krum, Sue Schommer, Laurie Stuben, Sandy Hubert, Linda Fentz, Mary Warner, Janice Peterson, Barbara Haas, Marsha Brotz, Dianne Desmond, Peachy Johnson, Mary Ellen Sloan, Kathy Krier, Rita and Ruth Aldakauskas, Carol Wimler, Margaret Funk, Jane Pfister, Mary Keppler, Claire Kilton, Margaret Jung, Liz Schultz, Nancy Peters, Laurie Strohschein and Connie Babitz.

Prange's Teen Club Float
Back to School Show
Bratwurst Day Parade
August 1963

Prange's Teen Club and Teen Board

Prange's Teen Board and Teen Club started about 1962 and 1964 respectively. A Girls Only organization, members of the Teen Board and Teen Club were style ambassadors to the community. They took classes on poise, learned how to properly dress and how to act as hostesses at parties. Members came from all over the county to participate. Teen Club meetings were held after school on Fridays at Prange's.

Teen Board members received one or two outfits from Prange's as part of their election to the board. For the first two years of the Board's existence each girl received two outfits of her own choosing, usually Bobby Brooks label. After that each girl received one of Prange's choosing, all the same color and style. Girls were required to wear these outfits to school on the day of a meeting or to a special event—Great advertising for Prange's! The girls were paid $1 per hour and received a 10% discount on clothing. Great deal for the girls.

The members of the Teen Board had a number of responsibilities each year. They served as hostesses for the Medical Auxiliary Fashion Show held at Pine Hills Golf Club every spring. Prange's provided the clothes and commentary. The Medical Auxiliary provided the models.

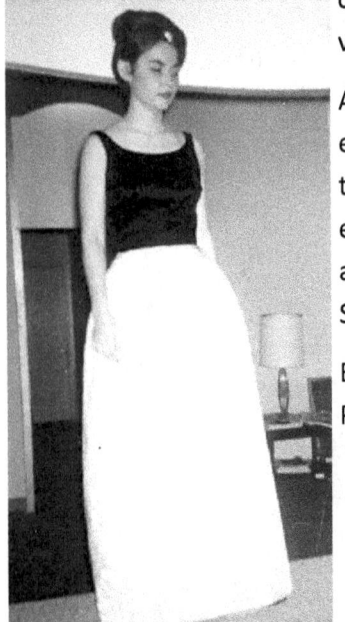

A huge fall back-to-school fashion show was held each August. The Teen Board/Teen Club provided the models and organization. Prange's provided everything else. This extravaganza was usually held at Urban Middle School or North or South High School.

Board members also rode on floats provided by Prange's for Fourth of July and Brat Days parades.

Photos, this page and opposite, Teen Board member and model Margaret Bushner.
Pine Hills, 1964

1940s
High School Debs Congregate in Prange's High School Shop

"Give high school girls what they want in clothes and make them feel perfectly at home in the junior department." That is the working theory of Prange's High School Shop.

Prange's finds out what they want from the girls themselves, for they feel that high school girls have excellent taste in clothes if left alone to select what they want. They, of course, know their price limitations and Prange's, of course, caters to all type of budgets.

Above: H.C. Prange record department where kids could listen to the newest in 45 rpms and 33 lps before buying them.

At Right: Seventeen Magazine Cover, 1963.

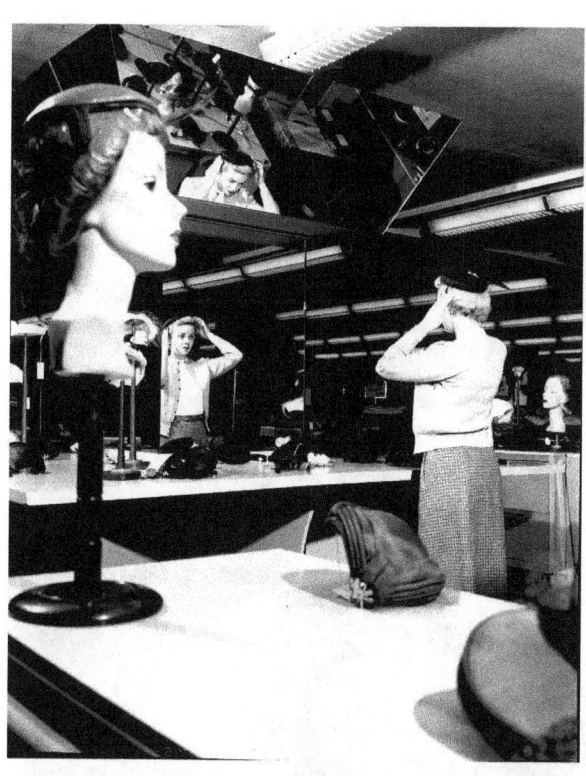

1950s Pricing
Chino Pants $2.98
Boys Shoes $4.95 1950
Nylon Stockings 2 pairs for a dollar
Men's Suits $45.00
Ladies Full Length Cashmere Coat $59.00
Men's All Wool Suits $28.90
Ladies Sandals $2.95
Men's Dress Shoes $13.98
Children's Shoes From $2.95
Short Spring Coats $9.88
Girls Dresses $2.98
Denim jeans $2.49
Boys shirt $1.10
Boys winter jacket $7.80
Leather Jacket $4.88
Men's shirt $3.99
Women's handbag $1.32

Hat Department, images at left and below.

Above: Anniversary Sale Women's Foundations

At left: Stairway to the basement restaurant

Train display often seen at Christmas in the Toy Department.

Men's Shave Shop
Razors, Cologne, etc.

Live Models

H.C. Prange frequently used live models in the stores. Models created public interest in buying products such as clothing, cosmetics, food, and housewares. The information they provided helped consumers make choices among the wide variety of products and services they sought to buy.

These same models also appeared in newspaper ads and print media advertising H.C. Prange products.

Above: Sue Frees in Women's Clothing.
Right: Sue Frees, White Stag Outfit, 1958.
Images on these two pages from the Frank and Sue Frees Reif Collection

Top Left: Bruce Nagourney, Susan Frees Reif and daughter, Kelly Reif– H.C. Prange Spring Bridal Show, 1966, "When Wedding Bells Ring"
Top Right: Susan Frees
Center Right: Susan Frees, Mademoiselle, 1958.
Left: South Side Junior High Style Show, L to R, Sue Frees, Connie Welsch, Ruth Schmidt, Deborah Gutoski

H. C. Prange Choir

This image of the H.C. Prange choir was taken during the 1960s. Members include Evelyn Hoegger, front row, fourth from left and photo donor; Norma Rautman, front row, second from right; Irene Rhines, front row, first on right; Mrs. Bishop, second row, first on right; Russ Roethel, fourth row, first on right; Don DeBelt, fourth row from front, far left; Jeff Braeger, third row, far left; Dennis Leffin, second row, far left.

Sunbeam Promotions Adventure

In early 1960 Prange employee Ron Klunk was sent to the Manitowoc Airport by Mr. Prange to pick up a lion cub for a Sunbeam snowblower promotion. Ron thought it would be a small cub, but it turned out to be a 150 pound, eight month old African lion cub, an animal the size of a large dog. The cub was in a cage in the plane, but in order to get the cage out of the plane, the cub had to come out of the cage and the cage had to be knocked down. So lucky, lucky Ron got to hold the very large lion cub on a leash until they could load him back into the cage on the truck.

On the trip back to Sheboygan, the truck broke down near Northeim. While the men waited in the dark with the stranded truck, the lion cub created quite a racket. A patrolling sheriff who stopped to help them call a wrecker noted the odd noises coming from their truck. When told it was a lion, he was skeptical. Surprise for him!

The lion stayed with Ron for a week, eating ground round and vitamins. Needing daily walks, Ron learned to keep that leash taut and at arm's length from his ankles, which quite often acted as playthings for the cub.

At week's end the cub was to return to Dayton, Ohio. But, officials from North Central Airlines refused to accept him as a passenger because of his size, so Ron once again brought him back to Sheboygan to await another way home.

Above and Below: Prange employee, Ron Klunk, with the lion cub used as part of a Sunbeam promotional campaign in the early 1960s.

Air Conditioning Makes Its Debut

September 7, 1960

The H.C. Prange Co. today announced plans to entirely air-condition its Sheboygan store. The project had been under consideration for some time. A 400-ton unit powered by two 360-horsepower electric motors will be used in the project. It will be one of the largest air-conditioning units in the state. Work on the project is already under way. Company officials said the project will not affect retail operations. The project is expected to be completed by June 1, 1961. The air conditioning unit, along with necessary related equipment, will be installed in a 40 by 100 foot penthouse to be constructed on the roof of the main Prange building. Leslie Quasius, president of Quasius Brothers Inc. , a Sheboygan construction firm, which holds the general contract for the project, said the total weight of the equipment in the penthouse will exceed 500,000 pounds, making it necessary to reinforce the existing columns of the building to carry the additional weight.

Smoke Stack Razed

March 28, 1962

Steeple Jacks started to raze the 125 foot smoke stack of the H.C. Prange Company powerhouse this week. The stack was built in 1912 and was used continuously until the company's new combination heat plant and air conditioning system was installed on the roof of the main building. The powerhouse and warehouse building will be removed to provide additional space.

February 1, 1963

Prange's Meat Department Goes Self-Service

New refrigerator cases, storage coolers, air conditioning and a packaging room have been added in the meat department . . . Five butchers and three packaging girls will be working in an immaculately white enamel cutting and packing room to out meat weighed and priced for the convenience of the hurried shopper. . . For those who prefer, there will be a butcher on duty at all times to tend to the personal needs of the customer.

March 16, 1964
Eighth Street Entrance Showcases Air Doors
The exterior of Prange's store was refaced with white brick and blue trim. It was a theme that was also used in the new Appleton and Green Bay stores. But, the most interesting feature of this remodel was the "air doors" of the North Eighth Street entrance. The doors remained completely open during business hours, all year around. Sliding doors were closed at night and during the worst weather, but otherwise they were open. (Everyone remembers the giant whoosh of hot air that met you when you went through the open doors.)

Though fun for kids and shoppers, the open air doors were extremely inefficient. They were eventually replaced with revolving doors. The large canopy over the front door was always a worry during winter snow storms - what if the weight was too much for the canopy to bear?– what if it collapsed? Ironically, after the fire, when the building was demolished and everything else fell down, the canopy remained standing. It was stronger than anyone knew. The image above was taken in August of 1973.

Shoe-fitting fluoroscopes were X-ray machines installed in shoe stores from the 1920s until the 1960s in the United States. The machine had steps for a child to ascend. The child would then place his or her feet in the opening provided and while remaining in a standing position, look through a viewing porthole at the top of the fluoroscope down at the x-ray view of the feet and shoes. The sales assistant observed the child's toes being wiggled to show how much room for the toes there was inside the shoe. The bones of the feet were clearly visible, as was the outline of the shoe, including the stitching around the edges. The exposure time would have been around 15 seconds.

The Prange shoe x-ray machine ceased to be used in the early 1960s.

H.C. Prange Christmas Windows

The H.C. Prange Christmas windows are probably the most talked about and fondly remembered aspect of the great department store. Sometime in late October of each year the big first floor windows would be covered to conceal the work going on behind them. The beautiful windows would be unveiled on Thanksgiving morning. Entire families would come to see the Christmas magic.

The windows were decorated beginning in 1940. A November 20, 1940 Press announcement said, "Beginning tomorrow, and throughout the Holiday Season, the Windows of Christmas City will X-ray the hearts of everyone you know. You will see them in the cherished desires of the tiny baby who cannot speak his thoughts, the dear old lady who says, "There is nothing I Want," and of all the people you know in between." Come and see these dramatic windows. Each one a great Heartful of Christmas. Gift ideas for everyone on your list. See the interior of Christmas City where making people happy is the chief industry.

Images: Kneeling down for a closer view of the toys in one of the famous Prange windows is little Mark Hlade, four year old son of Mr. and Mrs. John Hlade, Waukegan, Illinois.

With him is his uncle, Father Richard Cerpich, Milwaukee, and his older brother, Greg. The boys were visiting relatives in Sheboygan for the weekend and ,of course, were treated to a trip to Prange's.

During the war years there were no mechanical Christmas displays, but the windows were filled with toys and beautiful things that made great Christmas gifts.

The windows returned in November of 1948 when the Press announced, "In keeping with a tradition of many years our Christmas windows again radiate the excitement and loveliness of the season.

A huge circus train was center stage in 1950. Bruce the Talking Spruce appeared in 1972.

A new holiday attraction on Plaza 8 at Niagara Avenue appeared in 1976. It was Mrs. Santa in the Gingerbread House. Mrs. Santa made craft items and tree ornaments in her little house.

By 1981, Santa's arrival in Sheboygan was taking place at Memorial Mall.

Though one of the best loved memories of Prange's, they are probably the least photographed aspect of the entire department store. SCHRC has very few images of the famous windows.

Christmas 1967

Most Popular Games of 1967

Kerplunk
Johnny Astro
Talking G.I. Joe action figures
Mega Bloks, Newton's cradle
Uncle Fester's Mystery Light Bulb
Lite-Brite
Ants in the Pants Game
Ouija board

Important Happenings of 1967

The first handheld calculator was invented.
The largest Emerald, the 'Gachala Emerald' was found. It weighs in at 858 carats.
Rolling Stone began publication. The first issue sold about 5,000 copies.
Having been tested in a few outlets, 7-11's Slurpees became available in all locations in 1967.
Cost of a Superbowl ad in 1967: $42,000
South African doctor Christiaan Barnard performed the first heart transplant.

Billboard #1 Music Hits of 1967
I'm A Believer - The Monkees
Kind Of A Drag - The Buckinghams
Ruby Tuesday - The Rolling Stones
Love is Here and Now You're Gone - The Supremes
Penny Lane - The Beatles
Happy Together - The Turtles

Will Call Department

Shoppers could send their bundles from all over Prange's store to the Will Call Department where they would be stored until the shopper completed his/her duties. An attendant from Will Call would then carry the packages to the shopper's car. Will Call was like a drive-thru or drive-up service. Will Call was manned by older or disabled employees. The company was great about matching people with jobs that worked with their abilities and health concerns. The Will Call entrance was on the southeast side of the store. The photo above shows the Will Call entrance at Prange's in May of 1971.

Pipe Bursts, Damages Prange's Merchandise

Sheboygan Press December 31, 1973

A frozen sprinkler pipe that burst sometime Sunday morning caused an estimated $1,000 damage to merchandise in the H.C. Prange Co. store and brought virtually every piece of fire-fighting equipment rushing downtown. The incident was discovered shortly after 8 a.m. about two hours before the main store was due to open, and there were only a few dozen customers inside shopping in the grocery department at the rear of the store. The damaged merchandise, all software goods, consisted mostly of men's and women's clothing and sportswear. Most of the damage occurred downstairs as the water flooded down through the apparatus which operates the air curtain door at the store's main entrance on North Eighth Street. According to Henry Meyer, operations manager of the store, the frozen pipe should have contained an anti-freeze solution. Heat to that area had been turned off in order to conserve energy.

Prange's Renovation Underway . . . Expansion Elbows Out Grocery

Sheboygan Press
January 8, 1975

For the first time in local history, you can't buy a beefsteak or a can of beans in downtown Sheboygan. The winds of change veered into the H.C. Prange Co. grocery department, last week leaving the shelves bare and the city without a downtown grocery.

The Prange Company decision to close its grocery follows the exodus of the Schultz Sav-O Piggly Wiggly at 9th and Wisconsin in 1971 and before that, the downtown lost the A & P at 9th and Niagara. Last week's sales cleaned out the final grocery items and workmen now have taken over the department for renovation that should be completed by spring, Prange officials revealed.

"It was a difficult decision, but we're terribly crowded. This was the only food outlet in a total of our 17 department and discount stores. In this day and age, a complete grocery department should have more space than we were able to give to the operation," Gunther said.

Also, Gunther emphasized, "Groceries are not our main business and we need the area for expansion of other departments. "On the downtown area in general", Gunther said, "We agree with the Chamber of Commerce that another anchor department store on the former Penney corner is highly desirable."

What will be available to Prange food shoppers? "The delicatessen and bakery will be expanded," Gunther said, "and some new items are planned for the delicatessen." The first floor fountain-lunch counters will be continued and plans call for maintaining candy and tobacco, departments on a modified basis." Prange's will-call also stays.

Guenther said that shoppers will be able to obtain such quick-serve items as milk, butter, eggs, bacon, cold cuts, wieners, some frozen foods, hamburger patties and bratwurst (fresh and frozen) and the sausages and cheeses that find their way into all parts of the country as gifts.

The roasted turkeys and baked hams that have crowned many local holiday tables over the years will still come out of the Prange kitchens, Gunther revealed. A number of other food services also will be maintained. Eight stand-up freezers are among the items retained by the delicatessen in the sale of equipment, it was noted. How will the former grocery-meat area be used? Besides the enlargement of bakery and delicatessen, the first floor men's department will be expanded; jewelry, stationery, cards, hosiery, accessories and main floor sports wear will get more elbow room. Aisles will be shifted and a general up-dating and easing of the first floor operation are in the blueprints, Gunther revealed.

Staff "Relocated"

What has happened to the grocery employees? "Everybody has been relocated," Gunther said. Most of the staff was on a part-time basis, with a relatively small full-time crew, it was noted. Leslie Theune, who headed up the grocery, will manage the PW Prange Way discount operation in the downtown store. "I'm enthusiastic and looking forward to the challenge," Theune said of his switch. Stressing the positive aspects of the change, store officials said that services will continue over the remodeling period. "We will keep the high standards we have always had in the things we offer", Guenther concluded. Now the question, is the public reaction to this latest target of those winds of change blowing down 8th Street in this case altering daily patterns of living set nearly a century ago.

July 1979   Prange Post   PostScripts

A gala event was held at The Villager on May 23rd for retirees Rolean Leonhardt (carpets), Evelyn Hammes (domestics), Alvina Kahlbow (Drapery), Lillian Ranniker and Millie Roth (Books and Luggage), M.C'd by our own Maury Schmidt. Included in the entertainment was the debut of a new rock group, "The Babies," known to us as Jerry Wilson (furniture), Don Ehlert (Decoration), and Barb Hengst (drapery). There was a visitor from Carl -Nack-The Magnificent or as we know him, Carl TeWinkel (carpets). The grand finale featured "Wonder Women." Watch out Rockettes, here they come — Val Zier (drapery), Shirlee Riddle (Credit), Cheri McCracken (Secretary), Jane Clear (Secretary), Kay O' Donnell (decorating), Kathy Warburton (P-W Main), Debbie Nielsen (drapery), Judy Warburton (credit), Marie Raven (sportswear), Mina Ohlschmidt (Switchboard), Sharon Sandmire (management). "The Bubble Girls" were Vi Siemers-Hermann (retired), and Eileen Schieble (secretary). A monetary gift was presented to each of the honored guests.

Evelyn Hoegger (Sportswear) is most proud of her daughter, Jodine, age 15, who participated in the Miss Teenage Sheboygan on April 21 at the Horace Mann School. Jodine was awarded the Miss Citizenship Award.

March, 1980   Prange Post

H.C. Prange switched over from a manual billing system to a computerized system.

The Beginning of the End

Downtown Prange Store Evacuated
Floors Buckle After Water Main Breaks

Sheboygan Press May 4, 1983

Sheboygan's biggest department store was evacuated at mid-morning today after a break in an underground water main caused floors to sag. The incident at the H.C. Prange Company's nearly quarter-million square foot department store on Plaza 8 at Wisconsin Avenue, apparently resulted in no injuries, but forced closing of the store, at least for the rest of the day.

The break in the water main located under the four-story structure was noticed about 9 a.m., when employees reported seeing water in the basement. The water main rupture apparently undermined ground under the basement floor, causing support pillars around the building's escalator system to shift, according to Sheboygan Fire Battalion Chief Albin Suppanchick. That, in turn, resulted in upper floors sagging, as much as one to 1 1/2 feet.

Sheboygan fire fighters were summoned to the store at 10 a.m. to pump water from the basement, which houses a Prange-Way discount store. Suppanchick said water was standing two to three inches deep on the basement floor, although it was deeper in some areas. Several store employees reported flooding in the basement elevator shaft.

The pipe with the hole that caused the flooding and washout of the concrete columns in the basement of Prange's.

Suppanchick told The Press the floors—which are of poured concrete construction—buckled less than an hour after fire fighters arrived, in a 30-foot diameter area around the store's escalator system.

An employee of a local engineering firm, who was inside the building after the incident, said the basement floor dropped 14 to 15 inches near a support column where the water main had broken. Each floor above the support column had correspondingly sagged, he said. Customers in the store at the time said debris fell from the sagging ceilings as they were fleeing.

"I was on an escalator when I saw the ceiling cracking above the second floor," said Bonnie Hagan, an H.C. Prange Company employee. "It nearly hit a woman nearby, but she managed to jump back."

John Rusch, another Prange employee working in the fourth floor computer department said he heard a "rumble . . . and the next thing they told us to evacuate the building. Rick Horzen, who was working on the fourth floor at the time, said, "People were yelling for us to get out even before they could make the PA (public address system) announcement."

Base of Column N4 basement - looking South

The employees said there was no panic, but people were running to get out of the building. Police officials at the scene said they thought the customers were shaken by the experience and were comforted by police and store employees.

Prange spokesman Robert Wilson, vice president, declined to elaborate on the situation, saying only that the building had "structural problems"

"We are out of business for today," Wilson said. Suppanchick said there was no actual collapse of any floors, but he expressed concern that "the possibility" exists for a collapse.

Gas and water service to the building were shut off and engineering and architects were on the scene at midday to assess the extent of damage.

David Rudig, chief engineer with Miller Consulting Engineers, told *The Press* shortly after noon that an investigation will be made to determine the extent to which the building's support system has been overstressed. A structural computer program will be used to assist that study, he said. Rudig was confident that the damage could be repaired.

Encompassing 235,000 square feet, the H.C. Prange Company store was built in stages over the past 74 years. The first segment was constructed in 1909 and expansions were added in 1912, 1913, 1923, 1925 and 1926 with a major remodeling completed in 1965. It is the parent store of the retail chain which operates 42 Prange and Prange-Way stores in Wisconsin, Illinois and Michigan.

'Floors Were Sagging, My Heart Pounding

Sheboygan Press, May 4, 1983'

Judith Born was having a package wrapped this morning about 10:45 a.m. on the third floor of Prange's when she heard "a loud noise like something being dropped on the floor above. It went on for about a minute, and up there near the crystal everything tinkled, "she said.

"I'd noticed when I came in that the basement was closed off and they said it was because of water and mud from a broken main. The woman wrapping my present said that maybe it (the noise) was the new phone system being put in, up above. But then things started falling and sliding."

About 20 customers on the third floor were herded toward the outside walls of the building as the floors sagged near the center toward the escalators.

We said, "We've got to get out of here" Official looking people were running up and down the escalators. The escalator from third to second was still working at that point and we were escorted over to the escalators."

Born said she surmised people were not taken to the elevators near the outside of the building, because it looked as though they would have had to traverse damaged floor area to get them out.

Customers and employees were outwardly calm, she said, but as she walked the sloping floor toward the escalator, "my heart was pounding." Born said she looked to the support pillars in the sagging floor area and was afraid that the floors would collapse. "Also I saw hanging signs and things on the floor, and a mannequin looking like a dead person sprawled on the floor, her clothes flung out, and I thought, "I want to get out of here."

About 50 people were making their way down the escalators with her, Born said. Born noticed elderly women "coming down from the fourth floor beauty salon area with their hair in rollers and with towels around their shoulders, and I saw an employee helping one elderly woman walk down the escalator. Employees were very sensible about the whole thing, I think."

The customers walked the stopped escalator flight from second to first and were herded quickly out the front doors. "That was the only bad part," she said, "there were people there at the door trying to get in and the men were trying to tell them to stay away and they weren't listening. As I left, I told them to stay away.

People on the Plaza seemed unaware. Born marveled, "They were just browsing there and in the library." Born estimated there might have been about 100 people in the store at the time of the evacuation, "but that's only a guess."

Sheboygan Press   May 5, 1983

Prange Problems

Also affected by the sinking of the column was the store's escalator system. The steel framing for the escalators is connected to the flooring and it "deflected" as the floor shifted downward, according to reports.

Workmen had begun stabilizing of the first floor today by erecting large wooden columns in the basement. They were also in the process of breaking open the basement floor to get a better look at the area washed away by the accumulated water, according to reports.

Company officials were seeking office space for corporate officials as well as for the company computer operation. Its computer office, which serves all Prange Company stores, is located above Kress-Hertel Company, a half-block from the department store. . . . Prange Company Vice President Robert Wilson denied rumors which began circulating after the incident that the company had closed off an employee lounge area in the basement several days ago because of a structural problem.

Robert Culver, superintendent of Sheboygan's Water Utility, said the break was not in a city water main but in a Prange Company internal water system line. . . . .

Sheboygan Mayor Richard Suscha, who heard about the incident while in Madison Wednesday, said today that city officials have offered "all the services the city can muster" to aid Prange officials. "The Prange Company has been a landmark in downtown Sheboygan and we certainly hope that they will continue to be a landmark," Suscha said. . . .

Sheboygan Press   May 6, 1983
Prange Employees Hopeful, Optimistic

A remarkably positive attitude prevailed after H.C. Prange Co. officials met this morning with more than 400 employees of the firm's downtown store in the aftermath of Wednesday's accident which closed the building indefinitely.

Henry C. Prange, chairman of the board for the department store chain, fielded questions from employees after giving them as much information as the store's management had at the time. At one point, an employee even thanked Prange for his honesty and compassion in dealing with the unforeseen incident.

It was so wonderful of him to take time out from his busy schedule to meet with us, to treat us like human beings," said Faye Schilling, 7317 Shircel Road and employee in the Prange-Way housewares department said. . . .

James Bogolin, a Sheboygan resident who works in the bakery, said he was a bit worried about the situation. "I just hope the 30-day estimate before the store is reopened is most accurate," Bogolin said.

The employees' feelings may be best reflected in the line of questioning during the meeting with Prange, questions which dealt with how customers could pick up ordered merchandise or repaired items more than with how their lives could be affected by the accident. "That's not surprising, because to most employees at Prange's, the customer is Number One," Mrs. Schilling said.

Sheboygan Press   May 5, 1983
Damage Assessment Continues . . . Prange: 'We Intend to Stay'

Sheboygan's downtown retail anchor for nearly a century remained closed today but the head of the H.C. Prange Co. said today the department store chain 'has every intention' of continuing its department store operation in Sheboygan. . . .

Damage, however, was described as "major" by several who viewed the scene. Estimates on the length of time needed to complete repairs ranged from 30 days to as long as six to eight months, according to reports. . . .

About 450 employees of the downtown store are affected by its closing, according to the board chairman.

Prange said an effort will be made to provide work for the downtown store's employees at Prange-Way West, and in the downtown store, once its safety has been assured. Merchandise in the downtown store will be packed up and shipped to the firm's Green Bay distribution center for redistribution to other stores in the chain, and the downtown store's employees will be used to remove the merchandise.

In leaving the building as quickly as they did, many employees left personal effects behind. Merchandise on order for customers also remains in the store. . . .If the fire department approves, a system will go into operation to get employees; personal effects and customer merchandise, such as bridal dresses needed next weekend, removed. He invited employees to come to the store's north entrance at noon Monday to pick up their things.

. . Prange said the firm's corporate offices will be set up temporarily in the former Pemco Inc. plant office in the 2000 block of New Jersey Avenue and the downtown store's headquarters will be shifted to the Prange warehouse on Martin Avenue.

The photos of Prange's interior from the preceding page through page 105 were taken after the floor collapse. They were contributed by Quasius Construction. Quasius managed stabilization and clean-up of the site. Note the uneven floors and ceilings and crack in many of the images.

Sheboygan Press   May 13, 1983
Prange's Prefers Downtown, No Decisions Yet On Repair Or Replacement Of Crippled Store

M*A*S*H is alive and well and living in Sheboygan. . . . Sheboygan's M*A*S*H is the Mobile Accounting and Staff headquarters of the H.C. Prange Co. relocated from the fourth floor of the retail chain's downtown Sheboygan store to a temporary location at 2005 New Jersey Avenue, former home of Pemco Inc. The Prange M*A*S*H—the name dreamed up by an anonymous staffer with a sense of humor— is in full operation only nine days after a support pillar at the downtown store was undermined by water from a broken underground main, forcing the building's closure.

Sheboygan Press May 26, 1983

Prange's Planning New Downtown Store
Retail Giant To Raze 100-Year Old Outlet

Sheboygan's H.C. Prange Co. department store, the historic four-story retail giant that has anchored the city's downtown business district for virtually all of this century, will be razed. And rising from the rubble of the old structure that has been a dominant feature here for eight decades will likely be a new, modern 100,000 square foot department store "built for the decades of the 1980s and 1990s," Henry C. Prange, board chairman of the Sheboygan-based retail chain, told 350 employees of the old downtown store this morning. . . . Prange, at this morning's meeting at the St. Clement Parish Center, told the store's employees that repairing and reopening the 235,000 –square-foot facility simply isn't feasible.

While insurance would cover the cost of fixing the damage, he related, the cost of bringing the building's old electrical and water systems up to date would be at the company's expense and couldn't be economically justified. Almost as one, the employees groaned in dismay, then broke into delighted applause as Prange quickly went on to reveal a decision by the firm's board of directors, made late Wednesday, to build a new 100,000-square-foot department store in Sheboygan. . . . It will take until Spring or Summer of 1984 to complete the new facility.

Brief History of the Old Store
The H.C. Prange Co. store grew in the early part of this century to become as was advertised "Sheboygan's largest department store" and was so known statewide. As business expanded, various buildings and additions were built so the store eventually occupied six buildings and extended basements covering the best part of a square block. The first of the permanent buildings was four stories and basement just north of the alley. This was followed in 1922 with a four-story corner building which replaced several older, smaller buildings. The shoe department building was to the east and east of that the grocery building built in 1912 with entrance facing Wisconsin Avenue. These parts were separate buildings divided by heavy brick masonry walls with connecting openings at the main aisles.

A row of houses facing 7th Street lined the east part of the block in those days, and barns for horses and delivery wagons and sleighs were located on the north side of Wisconsin Avenue opposite the grocery department entrance.

The founder, Henry C. Prange, personally is to be credited with the large patronage among the people of the city and the county. He spent much time in the grocery entry greeting customers, many of whom he learned to know by name, and with them in German.

In the days before World War I, German was heard in the store nearly as often as English. The German colloquial expression, "Down By Prange's" came to signify the high regard of the community for Prange's as the downtown center of the city.

Farmers would bring their produce to the store and most everything they raised would be accepted. The sidewalk along Wisconsin Avenue would be pile daily with egg crates, bushels of apples, potatoes, cabbages and similar vegetables and fruit in season. A man spent full time out on this sidewalk receiving produce. An early architectural assignment was to plan the installation of a conveyor from the sidewalk to the basement to take filled square wood egg crates to the candling and processing room below the grocery department. The empty crates were returned to the sidewalk on the conveyor to be picked up when the farmer went home later in the day. The farmers were paid, not in cash, but with a "Due Bill" which they could use in the store to make their purchases. The due bill was a long slip with the owner's name and amount of credit at the top. As purchases were made in the various departments, they were listed and deducted until the amount of credit at the top. As purchases were made in the various departments, they were listed and deducted until the amount of credit was all used. Purchases were sent to a "will call" area so when ready to leave for home, everything could be picked up at one place. Rainy days when farmers could not work in the fields were especially busy in the store, as they came to town and made Prange's their headquarters for the day.

Eventually, son H. Carl Prange assumed charge of the business. One day in 1928, Stubenrauch received an order to plan the removal of a section of the dividing wall on the first floor between the grocery and shoe department buildings. That was the start of change, remodeling and expansion during the next 35 years to make over into a unified modern large department store building.

Wall removal proceeded until all original dividing walls were removed in all selling areas on all floors and replaced with steel columns and beams. The brick walls supported floor joists having bearing into the wall from buildings on both sides, so a system of double beams was used with columns between them to support the floors and roof. Along with wall removal, the basement was made three feet deeper and converted from storage to sales space. Basement work was done, a small section at a time over a period of several years, until eventually the entire building area was excavated. Columns and footings were rebuilt one at a time. A pair of heavy steel brackets was bolted to the column several feet above the basement floor. Temporary beams were placed under the brackets and shored up with wood timbers and jacks, house mover style. The old footing could then be removed, the area excavated and a new footing and column base put in place before moving to the next column in the row.

Shopping was continued in the store above without the public being aware of the hazards in undermining the building below them. As the basement was converted to selling space, this became the first Prangeway department with lower priced merchandise. New storage space was provided under the parking areas east of the store and south of the alley. Basement work continued until almost all of the entire square block was excavated.

Jacob Houmes was general contractor. Abe Heiden did the shoring and steel erection and Hans Sievers was the owner's supervisor for all of this work. It was my job to calculate and design all of the steel work and make details of all the remodeling. I spent many hours measuring, checking and verifying conditions. All proceeded smoothly without any mishap. Whenever welding was done and sparks were flying, Hans Sievers had a man standing watch constantly with pails of water and a fire extinguisher to guard against fire.

New basement sales space required new basement stairways and then escalators were installed to the second floor, the first in the city. Escalators were so well accepted that they were relocated a few years later to the second and extended to the third and then to basement and fourth floors.

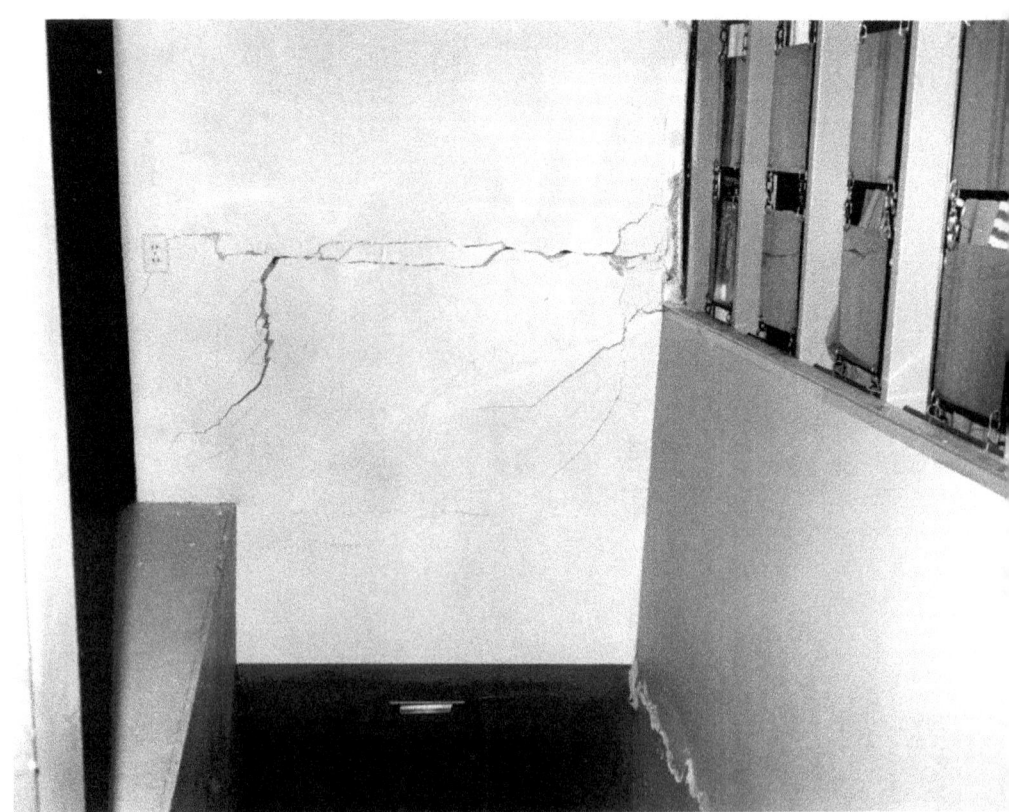

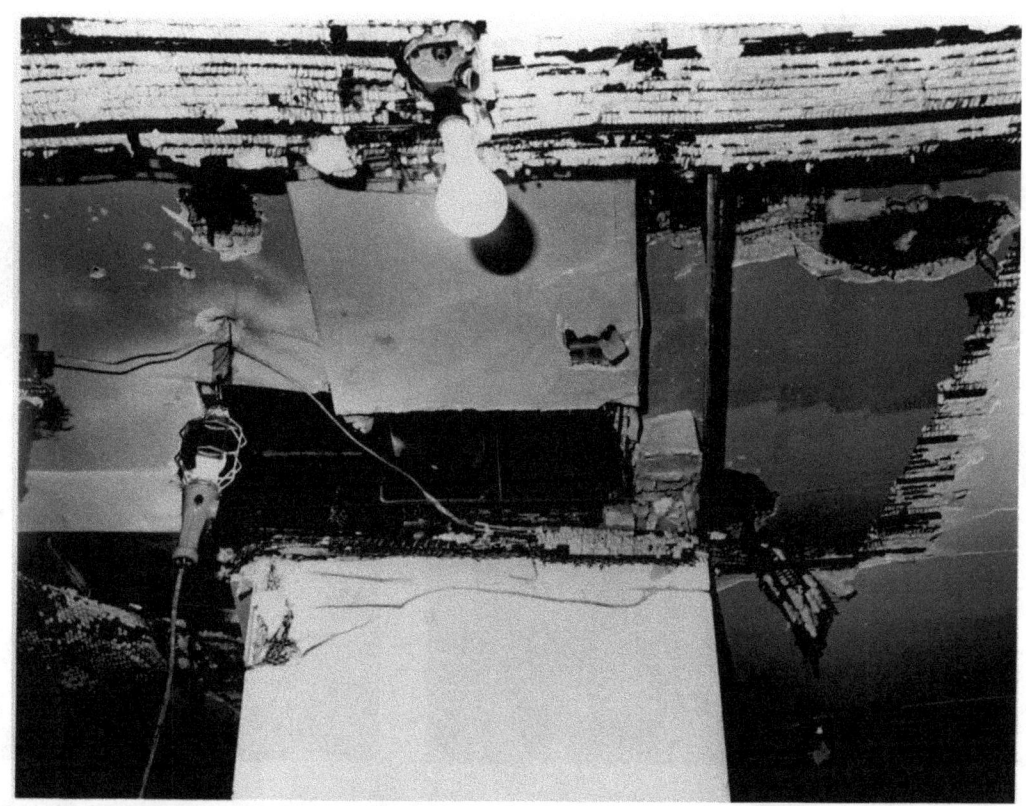

escalators - Looking Northeast
2ND OR THIRD

The End of An Era

H.C. Prange ablaze– Above left, the Eighth Street entrance. Above right, looking south at the corner of Wisconsin Avenue and Eight Street. Below, fire and smoke billow far above Mead Public Library as Prange's burns (Frank Reif images).

Fire at Prange's guts vacant store

A massive fire that filled the night sky on Sunday evening, October 16, 1983, hastened the demolition of the H.C. Prange store in downtown Sheboygan. The fire engulfed a full city block with flame as winds gusted to 25 miles per hour. Arson was suspected.

Starting about 7:30p.m. the fire, which raged for more than two hours, could be seen from fifteen miles away. Firefighters from seven departments and all three Sheboygan shifts fought the blaze. Because of the strong winds embers created fire hazards city residents were encouraged to soak their roofs with hoses to prevent further fires.

The focus of fighting the fire was on preventing the spread of the fire to the City Hall annex (old Mead Library), St. Clement's Church and school, the Kohler Arts Center and many residences. Major damage was done to the gym at St. Clement's but no other fires started. The Kohler Fire Department battled the blaze at St. Clement's where the roof of the gymnasium was completely burned through and the floor extensively damaged from water.

A large crowd gathers to watch the end of an era as the H.C. Prange department store burns to the ground.

The Prange store was in the process of being torn down by Buteyn Excavating and Grading and should have been completed within a week or two, after which construction on the new store was to have begun. Employees from Buteyn and Quasius Construction arrived on the scene within minutes of the alarm being raised and moved valuable equipment out of harm's way.

The Salvation Army sent 20 volunteers to the fire scene. They remained through the night serving food and beverages to the firefighters. Refreshments were provided by Fredericks Bakery, McDonalds and Verifine Dairy.

A pall of thick smoke hung over the city the next day as firefighters continued to pour water onto the smoldering remains of the building. Firefighters monitored the site because it was feared the exterior walls might tumble on to Plaza Eight. By mid-morning crews were on the scene to attempt to push in the southwest corner of the structure. They buckled and cracked making for a very unsafe situation.

Within one week of the fire arson was declared the cause. A $5,000 reward was offered for information leading to the capture and arrest of the arsonist.

The morning after the massive Prange department store fire crews remained to spray water on the smoldering fire. Smoke billowed from the piles of rubble as onlookers took it all in, another odd chapter in the demise of the great H.C. Prange department store.　　　　　　　　　　　　　　　　Leo Mueller images

A number of leads were investigated. A small group of young people was reported to have been seen at the site earlier in the evening. There was a report of someone being seen running from the scene at the time of the fire. And the oddest incident involved the discovery of a bicycle at the scene minus its owner. The Sheboygan man, whose bicycle was found at the scene, was reported missing a few days later. To date nothing has come from any of these early leads. The Prange arson remains one of Sheboygan's great mysteries.

Above, Another view of the smoking rubble of the H.C. Prange building taken from Wisconsin Avenue looking south. (Leo Mueller image)

Left, View of H.C. Prange rubble from Mead Public Library property looking east (Frank Reif image).

The Final Chapter

The end of the "old" Prange's started with the freak water main burst that caused irreparable structural damage to the 250,000 square foot department store in May of 1983. In October of that same year an arson fire gutted the empty building.

The company rebuilt on the same site, but the new store had only 97,000 square feet in one story and never had the same feel or connection to the city as the old facility.

H.C. Prange Co. showed profits until 1989 when Prange's acquired 117 specialty stores and took on large debt before the recession of the 1990s. The expansion and the recession took its toll on the company.

The headquarters for the chain was moved from here to Green Bay in 1990.

The company sold its Prange Way discount chain to a group of former executives in September 1990. The company was sold to Younkers in 1992. H.C. Prange and its subsidiaries consolidated as American Specialty in October of 1996 following a Chapter 11 bankruptcy reorganization.

Everyone's favorite company was gone, but certainly not forgotten. Here we are, decades later still reminiscing about 'all things Prange.'

Memories

Gloria Heisdorf, Elkhart Lake, Wisconsin

My earliest memories of Prange's go back to childhood. Four of us would pile into the back seat of our Ford, especially to view the animated scenes in Prange's windows. Little did I know at age five or six that I would work in that fine store some day. Prange's was "top shelf" in Sheboygan. Our family could not always afford to purchase at Prange's as their goods were a little pricey for my parents' budget.

Eventually, when I earned money of my own, I'd go "down by Prange's" for some nice things. In 1956, I decided I wanted a better paying job so I applied at the office of H.C. Prange Company. They hired me part-time which suited me fine.

I began as a cashier. People came in to pay cash or use a "due bill" on their account, put money on a lay-away or cash a check. "Due Bills" were given to farmers by the grocery department for produce (eggs, strawberries and raspberries, etc. in season) the "due bill" could only be applied to the farmer's account or used for Prange's products.

I was pretty nervous during the first few weeks, getting to learn all the procedures, especially the lay-away machine. The first day I had just learned the basics when a lady came in with a fist full of lay-away items. She had fifteen items and wanted to put fifty cents down on each one. That meant fifteen separate transactions. I remember praying that I would enter all of this without error. I hadn't learned how to correct a mistake and I did manage to get each entry correct. I thought that if this happened every day I would go nuts in a big hurry.

As time went along, my nerves settled down and I don't recall another lay-away transaction like that one. After a few weeks I was asked to work in the "Cash Cage". More to learn. The "cash cage" was the employees' description of a special room about the size of a small bedroom. Four women were literally locked in this room that received all the cash from the sales clerks. Each of us had a small work area with a coin counting machine which looked like a large colander. Each morning all of the money from the various departments in the store came to us in separate envelopes. The currency and checks were counted by hand and the coins were dumped into the counting machine. We handled a lot of money.

At the end of the day we had to arrive at the total tallied by the sales clerks. Sometimes the clerks made mistakes. In any case, we had to find the error. I thought it was a very responsible job and I was paid 93.7 cents per hour. This was better than 75 cents at my previous job. After a few months Prange's increased my wage to $1.00 per hour.

The "cash cage" girls started work at 8 a.m. So we could get a head start counting money. The store was open, but not for business until 9:30 a.m. If we arrived early, we could browse around the store before customers arrived. Such temptations! Many spent their small wages in a hurry.

The prices in 1956 were far less than they are today, but so were our wages. I worked at Prange's for a few years until my husband needed some assistance in his insurance office. Once again I had to brush up on my bookkeeping skills. Numbers were not my forte. I will never know why I accepted such jobs.

Doris Klessig Wright, Marietta, Georgia

I grew up on a Manitowoc County dairy farm near Cleveland, the daughter of Edwin Klessig. All five Klessig children went to Central High School in Sheboygan.

In the 1930s I remember my father selling bushels of apples to the buyer at Prange's. The payment was in due bills which my mother enjoyed using! The heavy man who did the buying trusted my father to have quality apples throughout the bushels, not just the top.

I also remember the excitement of the first escalators at Prange's and seeing my foot bones in the X-ray machine.

Prange's was an important part of my growing-up years.

Judith Piper, La Mesa, California

On one of my pilgrimages back to Sheboygan, my cousin called me to say that Prange's was burning. We agreed to meet downtown to watch the blaze with a sizeable group of on-lookers. We watched as a little bit of town history and a lot of personal memories smoldered and sent black smoke into the twilight.

Prange's was the meeting place for all of us at one time or another. Prange's was a place to buy your first Mother's Day purchase and where you could try coffee. They had the best sour cream muffins I ever tasted and I still wish I had their recipe. I had my first rides on an elevator, escalator and had a chance to see my foot bones in the shoe X-ray machine. My first formal dance dress came from Prange's and I shopped there until the end on my yearly trips back home. Every Christmas season my mom would take me to the display of Santa's workshop. We could watch peppermint canes coming out of the elves' machines. It was a great place in Sheboygan memorialized by the phrase, "Down By Prange's".

Chuck Berg, Oostburg, Wisconsin

After walking through the doors of Prange's and receiving a warm blast of air from the heating grates on the floor, my mother and I made our way to the escalators . . . Pretty cool stuff to a little boy in the late 1960s. While traveling down the escalator to the basement to shop at Prange Way. This little boy wondered what would happen if he didn't step off the escalator as the last step disappeared. What happened is the bottom of his snow boot was pulled into the escalator causing an emergency stoppage.

The snow boot was the typical fashion for that era: black, shin-high with a chrome zipper extending through the middle from the bridge of the foot to the top of the boot. The deed caused quite a commotion that brought store clerks running and eventually a trip to the store manager's office for an explanation. Mom always said, "Honesty is the best policy so I told the truth and waited to suffer the consequences of wanting to satisfy my curiosity. To my surprise there was no punishment and no lectures. Instead, the store manager apologized for what had happened and walked my mother and I to the shoe department. He told us to pick out any pair of boots we wanted and that they would be "on the house." While I gleamed at a pair of those, green, knee-high rubber boots with the tan bottoms and yellow shoe strings, my mother explained to me we would be replacing the boot with the same type that were wrecked and not a more expensive pair.

Given the atmosphere of today's world, my favorite part of that Prange's memory goes beyond the store itself and into the hearts of the people: my mother, the sympathetic store clerks and the store manager. More concern was shown for the well-being of a customer than for the condition of a piece of equipment. And the affected customer did not attempt to file a lawsuit for a huge sum of money because of mental anguish suffered by the experience. No new signs were posted explaining to people that it may be detrimental to their health to place body parts into a moving escalator. Simpler times . . . Perhaps better times. Lest we forget.

Mary E. Schetter Meyer, Kohler, Wisconsin

When I was a student at the UW-Extension in Sheboygan Falls in 1962-63 I got a weekend and evening job at Prange's as an elevator operator. This was just before the self-service elevators were installed. My job was to stop at a floor and call out, "Up please, going up" or "Down please, going down" and then ask the passengers, "Floor Please?" We were ever so polite!! It always amazed me how quiet people were on the elevator. All talk ceased until the door opened and people got out. Soon the elevators were switched to self-service and the public was left to fend for themselves. I moved to Accounts Payable. My pay was $1.12^{1/2}$ cents per hour. Today nobody could imagine working for that pay, but back then it was fair.

I was engaged to be married and my fiancé and I spent hours picking out household items at the store. I remember walking down 8th Street with Richard carrying the ironing board and I had the iron. Another day he carried the floor mop and broom and I had the set of kitchen stirring utensils. We thought it was great fun. Of course, we registered for wedding gifts at Prange's and the next big purchase was my wedding gown and my sister's bridesmaid dress. After we married I continued to work at Accounts Payable on the 4th floor and; I was working the day President Kennedy was assassinated. We were all listening to the radio broadcast in sheer disbelief and during that day I cashed a bad check—the first and last time that happened to me. I learned a valuable lesson in keeping my attention on business even during a national tragedy.

Prange's was a full service operation. There was a hair salon, photo studio, furniture and rug department, fine and casual clothing, housewares, sporting goods and even the bargain basement where the markdowns were "quality" items at low prices. There was an excellent restaurant and deli. One year I requested a Prange cherry cheesecake for my birthday instead of a regular cake. My mother-in-law bought it for me and was it good! There was also a grocery department and "will call" so that you didn't have to shop carrying loads of bags. Lay-a-way made it possible to buy items with low monthly payments, especially useful at Christmas time. The day after Christmas meant the annual ornament sale. I went almost every year and I still have a nice collection of ornaments. But the most important Prange item was, of course, the Charge-a-plate and I made use of mine.

After Memorial Mall opened on the west side of town, trips to the store were fewer while trips to Prange Way near the mall increased. Still, Prange's was such an integral part of Sheboygan life that it was difficult when they sold out. Other stores have come and gone in Sheboygan, but none had or will have the long lasting effect of Prange's. My great grandmother took eggs to Prange's with a horse and buggy and bought groceries with her due bills. Both of my grandmothers shopped at Prange's. My mother and then my sisters and I all shopped at Prange's. It was our hometown store and we shopped, "down by Prange's" for generations. Today Prange's memory has become a kind of community "glue" that keeps us connected as we reminisce about our Prange experiences. I am happy to have been a very small part of the Prange working family and happy to share my memories with you.

Marilyn Huenink Pitcher, Sheboygan Falls, Wisconsin

Younkers Should Revive Spirit of Old Prange's
Originally printed in the Sheboygan Falls News

Where did the old Prange's signs go? Are they tucked away in storage? Are they dismantled and recycled? Where are they now?

Memories are not disposed of so easily We cannot deposit them and forget their existence. It really isn't hard to accept Younkers because Prange's, the store I loved, "died" along with the old building Even downtown Sheboygan died a little when we could no longer go "by Prange's." I literally mourned its passing. It was a serious attack of nostalgia, a painful longing for things that used to be.

I slip back into the 1940s when I got my first job at Prange's. How exciting, but intimidating! The store bustled with activity and sound. It was the Christmas season and customers jostled one another, pushing toward the merchandise, especially on Friday nights. Bells clanged for supervisors, elevators banged, charge tubes clacked, registers pinged, babies cried, teenagers giggled. Clerks safely behind the counters, scurried around, giving advice, making sales, and wrapping gifts. I remember floor walkers, end-of-month sales, cherry Cokes after school, the basement store, the shoe X-ray, the will-call department and that wonderful, wonderful balcony overlooking the food areas. I remember "meet you in the shoe department" as families scattered in all directions.

My first assignment was in Drugs and Cosmetics. I can still visualize the exact locations of Coty lipsticks, Heaven Scent cologne, jeweled compacts, gigantic dresser sets, shaving brushes and, of course, Lydia Pinkham's Vegetable Compound. I never did know its purpose.

Three generations of my family clerked "by Prange's." I still use the Sunday-best dishes that my mother purchased when she sold china on the third floor. My first sale, an Old Spice gift set, was made to her so I could put the receipt in my scrapbook. My daughter's graduation dress and Teen Board photos nestle safely in my cedar chest.

It's hard to believe that Prange's lives only in my mind. Very vividly, I can see both H.C Prange and his wife walk the aisles, always polite, friendly and unassuming.

I wish I could take my grandchild to see the windows on Thanksgiving afternoon just to watch the wonder in her eyes. And then just before Christmas I'd like to take her to marvel at the religious scenes in those same windows.

Thank you, Prange family, for the job you provided throughout my Mission House years, for the magnificent anniversary and spring sales that helped to clothe my children, for the gloriously decorated windows, and the pleasures of Prange's. Now we welcome Younkers and are glad that you are here.

Carl Toepel, Howards Grove, Wisconsin

During the 1960s I taught at Urban Junior High School in Sheboygan. Many times in early morning on my way to work, I would stop at the Prange store to deliver rindawurst (beef sausage) for my father, Theodore Toepel, who with Nelson Kuhn, made the rindawurst at the Howards Grove Meat Market.

The Prange store with the friendly employees in each department, escalators, Christmas displays in the windows and having groceries, clothes, toys, etc. all in one store was a major part of Sheboygan history. The Prange store was the Macy's of the Midwest.

Lois Anderson, Stewartville, Minnesota

After working at various positions within the H.C. Prange store, I was fortunate enough to get a transfer into the Display department. This was the best job ever!

Back in the Display room my first job was to paint plain white plastic signs with a roller—dozens of them. We assembled dozens of bamboo birdcages. "On the floor" we used all sorts of props. As well as showing off garments, filmy scarves, handbags and jewelry draped off them. Anyway, that was artistic. It was my job to lug and put up displays high up above the rest of the store, near the ceiling. I carried a ten-foot ladder to each display to do my work I was amazed at the labyrinth of extension wires laying above the ceiling tiles, that I used to have to remove to secure the displays.

La Verne Hasenstein was experienced in that she knew the newest fashions, she would choose the newest and most expensive items to display. They were displayed on wheels, birdcages, whatever props we had. A wire cutter and a roll of wire and pliers were helpful in securing the items.

Mr. Stevenson had purchased props on his travels. His trips to Chicago always brought new ideas.

The front windows displayed the newest fashions on Eighth and Center Streets. There were seven mannequins, "expensive, but they didn't eat much," we always said. They stood in all sorts of stances. With a rod to hold them erect. To dress them with a pair of slacks usually meant that we would have to cut a hole in the slacks to get them on the rod. The mannequins sold many "Cruise Wear" swim suits in the middle of January.

Sometimes the manufacturer of the product sent their whole advertising package. We could display it as we wanted. The "Estee" line of perfume was the line that was the most expensive. The Estee Company sent us an original dress of filmy material, of floral design, that we were to dress the mannequin with. I drew the design, bought the material in the fabric department and sewed a dress like the original. Whenever we displayed perfume in the front windows we used "dummy bottles" of alcohol. The Lancôme line of perfume seen from outside was filled with alcohol, not perfume as you would imagine. There was no heat in the windows and we had to be careful of anything that may freeze.

As display persons we had to take care of the crystal chandeliers, too. They lit The Crystal Room, which sold only ball gowns and the most elegant of elegant clothing. Even dresses like the one worn by our own Miss Sheboygan in the Miss America Pageant. We kept those chandeliers sparkling with a cleaner from Germany.

A full page ad appeared in the Sheboygan Press advertising the silver lame dress. Actually, there were only three dresses in the total group of the Prange stores.

In the display department we cut out and made signs, covered boards for departments with velvets, moirés, taffetas, white goods. We were allowed to be original in our designs for the department to promote the merchandise.

The array was endless. One week a backdrop could be black and the next week it would be painted over with other colors or draped with some display to interest. Our goal was to excite the customer enough to purchase it. When a customer wanted an item from a display we were paged and asked to get the item for the customer

One of our most eye-catching displays was a Bistro table with a Bistro chair displaying 1828 jewelry. It was expensive imitation jewelry, but beautiful. The jewelry was so beautiful I am sure that some of the pieces are worn today.

Often when we thought we had the best looking display on our models, Mr. Stevenson would look at it and say it was not "Schlock" enough. We always needed to think "outside the box" to draw the cust-tomer's eye to the display.

But imagine, working in the Display department and being able to do the Christmas windows. As soon as the Anniversary Sale was over we put up curtains (No Peeking) and the elves, fellow workers and I, began putting together the animated characters.

We helped to create and capture the Joy of Christmas through the placement of characters behind the curtain to be unveiled on Thanksgiving Day.

The black curtain would remain and the anticipation from passers-by grew . . .

We placed animated ice skaters that went round and round on mirrored ponds and characters in Victorian dress played with sleds. A "Home Sweet Home" scene of animated people glancing into cupboards, baking, placing presents under the tree, were set into place. Tinseled miniature trees were decorated with German ornaments. The scene had a dramatic back drop of Theater paper, rolls and rolls of cotton for snow. Sparkling snow was sprinkled everywhere.

Christmas music and carols completed the scene.

Of course, there were other things that had to be done, too. Out "on the floor" we hung Christmas boughs and imitation Christmas candies, and set up all sorts of displays. There were twenty-six Christmas trees to be decorated. Green trees, white trees, little trees and those with new ornaments, and those that had ornaments that need to be redone. Strings of lights of every color sometimes became tangled and were a challenge.

Prange Way became Christmas Wonderland. We built a barn for the reindeer. It was so much fun. The outside was designed like a regular barn, with the half door entry. The inside was painted black and each reindeer had its own stall. There were dimly lit lights shining on each reindeer, including Rudolph. Their names glowed in the dim light. A line was painted on the floor leading to the Reindeer's stalls.

All the new toys were lined up on the way to the barn. That was an awe inspired display for me. Then beyond Dasher, Dancer, Prancer and Vixen, etc. . . . A velvet walkway lead to Santa Claus. All very secluded. And there the children secretly told Santa their wishes.

Beyond that was the "Children's Only Shop." Clerks helped children pick out gifts that they could afford and wrapped each one in wait for Christmas.

The talking Christmas tree on the first floor— Bruce the Talking Spruce— knew secrets of many of the children talking to them . . . simply because the clerks knew some of the families who frequented the store. One of the clerks often went behind the scenes and talked to some of the children. They believed in the talking tree . . . Who wouldn't?

At last, Thanksgiving Day had arrived. The adults and children with rosy cheeks gasped in joy as the curtains were pulled back to reveal the long-awaited H.C. Prange Christmas window displays.

It was the tradition. As crowds had traveled from miles around made gasps of oohs and aahs, you might think it was the Fourth of July, other than the Thanksgiving night air and warning of snow. The excitement of the Christmas season was electric and displayed on the spectator's faces.

They had come to see all the animated characters in motion to the Christmas music.

The grand finale came the week before Christmas when the delicate and very beautiful Christmas nativity scene was added to complete all Christmas anticipation and heart felt wishes from the H.C. Prange store. It was another blessed Christmas at Prange's.

After Christmas we delicately stored the animated characters and nativity scene in their wooden crates for the following year.

As all good things come to an end. Eighth Street was rebuilt. A water feature was added to the plaza. The windows were covered over with brick. Budgets were cut and the Display Department was disbanded.

After the demise of the Display Department I was transferred to Corporate Collection. The day I walked into the Corporate Collection office, I announced, "Here I am, teach me everything you can." Thus began a great education with the H.C. Prange Company.

As authoring supervisor I soon had my own team In those years the authorizing was done individually from the information in the files of customers who had filled out charge card applications. A formula was used to give the card holder permission to purchase the item on the floor. Some were denied. Bills were generated from the office of Jake Mueller who placed the sign over his office entrance stating "Under These Portals Enter the Best Billing Clerks in the World."

The Data Processing Department was in its early years. H. C. Prange Corporate Collection generated computerized letters to its delinquent customers. Grey bar paper was used to print all computer input.

One night when there were just two of us in the office, the Sturgeon Bay office requested some information. Not being familiar with the technology of a computer, the computer began to print. The paper printed and printed. Reams and reams of paper zigzagged to the floor, until a whole box of computerized paper lay on the floor. The two of us laughed and laughed. I think it was a laugh of embarrassment because neither of us thought of shutting the computer off.

Soon after, in another place of employment, as I was sitting at my desk on of my co-workers came in crying. She explained that H.C. Prange Store had a water main break and the store was unsafe to enter. As she spoke, it crumbled. She had previously purchased the dress for her daughter's wedding and it was waiting to be altered. It was hanging in the store that she could not enter. She did eventually get the dress in time for the wedding.

The fifteen years I spent with H.C. Prange were invaluable, not only from the education I received, but the many friends I gained. The customer was always right and service was everything.

Lois Anderson, Stewartville, Minnesota

Anniversary Sale 1960

"Lois, get a pop case and look out the window. It is like the County Fair." said Lee Nehrling. Lee was the head of the Receiving Department and was already watching the lines form and move with excitement on the streets below. Unlike myself, Lee was only too familiar with what the big sale had in store for us for the day. Ladies were attired in hats and gloves, not the varied blue jeans customers we see now. Some wore high heels. They were dressed for serious shopping. The Anniversary Sale was an adventure for me.

Just hours before the big anniversary sale, skits were played out by various clerks or actors as we called them. They demonstrated the right and wrong way to approach and help the customer. At Prange's, we were taught to stay with the customer and seek out what he/she was looking for to make them feel comfortable in their purchase. After the transaction, the receipt was to be stapled to the top of the H.C. Prange logo bag with the printing to the inside so that a lady would not smudge her gloves. Serving the customer was imperative. "The customer always comes first" was the Prange motto.

As we watched from the second floor north window looking down on Eighth and Center we saw people parking, jostling and shoving to get into line waiting for the store to open. It was the first day of the Big Anniversary Sale, the Prange Anniversary Sale.

With my expertise in sewing, I had just been hired to replace misprinted clothing labels. Labels that were misprinted as H.G. Prange instead of H.C. Prange. The labels which needed replacing were in hundreds of sweaters . . . The same sweaters which were going to be one of the big items for the Anniversary Sale.

Lee advised us to go down the escalators and watch as the crowds pushed closer and closer to the doors. As the doors opened, the shoppers flowed in. We watched them go hurriedly to the department of their choice. Many of them carried pillowcases to hold all their purchases. When the pillowcases were heavy laden they rushed to their cars, unloaded their merchandise and rushed back for more items. The excitement was contagious.

Department managers were beaming. The race was on!

Managers took tallies of their sales throughout the chaotic day. Behind the scenes, shoe stretchers (a broom handle and a damp cloth) stretched shoes that needed persuasion. Clerks were rushing from their stock rooms to replenish the shelves with blouses, jewelry and varied 'famous label' items. In a hurry to show jewelry to customers, gold necklaces became tangled.

The Cosmetic Department enticed their customers with "free fragrance samples." Yardley's fragrances wafted through the department. In the grocery department, angel food cakes, pillow doughnuts and rum cakes were specialties on sale.

There were so many specials, one could not get to all their favorite departments on the first day. Maybe the items would not be there on the next day of the sale. It would be a gamble to wait. The lunch counter was no exception with special prices for the sale. A line formed early at the lunch counter where the waitresses were efficient and friendly. The waitresses brought hot water for those customers who brought their own tea bags to dunk.

The Shoreroom Restaurant, in the lower level, was busy as well, with specialties of Prange's own Sour Cream Muffins, Macaroni Salad and their famous Prange Shrimp Salad. The food was delicious and the customers were happy to rest their feet before continuing on with their shopping.

To help ease the load for customers, Prange's offered home delivery for shopper's purchases. They also offered a 'will call' service, in which customers could have their packages safely stored, in trade of a 'claim' number, to gather their purchases at the end of the shopping day.

As the sale came to an end, the clerks took a deep breath and knew it was another successful Anniversary Sale. What an experience it was!

Memories
As I reflect, there were so many things with stood out about Prange's. A few of those are:
Shoppers in hats and gloves
Buyers who came into the receiving room to use employees as a sounding board for some of the incidents on the floor.
The farmers who brought in a pair of overalls from WWII Era with the government price freeze label on. Asking for a refund in 1960. The ticket on the overalls was $4.98. He got a refund. He said they didn't fit.
The buyers who would come to check if their merchandise had arrived from the garment districts in New York and the whoosh of the steam machine used to remove all the wrinkles from garments.
The wonderful smells of the bakery wafting up through the vents in the parking lot.
The fragrances which were tucked into monthly statements.
Clerks being so glad that a customer asked to check in the back room for an item, so they could sit down and put up their feet for a second or two.
Refunds with a smile.
The telephone operators at the switch board.
Storage of furs in the refrigerated storage room.
Associates eating their bag lunches in the fourth floor lunch room and watching the happenings on Eighth Street.
The department Christmas parties behind the scenes where the best manicotti was served.

The cot used by women when they were not feeling well.

The balcony over the grocery store to sit and eat lunch.

Inventory with various groups helping out on the day of inventory.

The therapy sessions as we called them, talking over the rounders or racks of garments before the store opened. We solved most of the world's problems during those sessions.

Departments which disappeared
Millinery department with veiled hats and finery
Wedding mantilla head pieces
Interior decorating
Candy and Nut counter
Grocery Store
Photography shop
Bridal shop and storage
Fur Storage
Alterations
Will Call
Prange Delivery Trucks
Lay A Way
The Display Dept.
The Eighth Street Windows
The Magical Christmas Windows

Kathleen Bub Walker, Chesterfield, Missouri

My memories of Prange's include many members of my family since many were employed at the store. My grandfather, Henry Bub, was for many, many years a clerk in the Hardware Department. Before that he spoke of delivering to customers using a horse drawn buggy. His brother, Charles Bub, was employed at Prange's for 48 years beginning in March 1893. Henry's brother-in-law, Otto Fenn, was also a long-time employee. My dad, Ray Bub, worked as a watchman where he was a young man and later as a baker. His brother, Elmer Bub, another long-time employee of Prange's ended his career as the head of the Receiving Department.

The annual Christmas window display was always an exciting time for young children. As I recall, the first display would be on Thanksgiving Day, late in the afternoon. The first taste of Christmas for all of us! The animated displays were such a wonder for everyone!

My first job was in the Bakery Department when I was in high school. While working one Saturday I lost my Central High class ring (1951) that I had just received. We checked everything, all the trash containers, swept the floor, checked the bakery trays, but no ring. I was resigned to the loss.

Then, several months later one of my fellow workers called to me that a customer had found a ring! She asked me to identify it, which I did, including my initials, KB, inside the band. My ring had been returned! Apparently when I placed a cake in the cake box my ring had slipped off and fallen into the box. The customer put the box, intact, into her freezer. When she finally removed the cake some months later, she found the ring and returned it to Prange's Bakery Department and to me! I still have that ring.

Later I came back to Prange's for a part-time job while attending Sheboygan Business College. I worked in the Accounts Payable Department on the 4th floor on the 8th Street side. From the windows we could look down on 8th Street. During the Centennial celebration in August of 1953, we watched several parades, including the one I photographed from above. I have two photos from that parade which I am enclosing. Quite a view!

Two years after the Centennial I was married and moved away. However, it was always a necessary to shop at Prange's when we returned to Sheboygan to visit family. Favorite bakery items were the cream-filled coffee cake (my favorite) and the frosted snails that my father-in-law liked.

I always had a feeling of loss when the building was replaced with the current building and then later when even the Prange name was no longer there. An important part of Sheboygan history was gone forever.

Patricia Adamavich, Sheboygan, Wisconsin

My earliest memories growing up in the 1940s and 1950s are, of course, the Christmas windows and x-ray machine in the shoe department, but also the elevator with a real person running it, the escalators and revolving doors in front of the store.

As a teen I remember playing records in a booth before you bought them, annual signing in front of the store from 1963 to 1968.

As secretary to the vice-president and general merchandise manager my duties were always interesting. The first thing in the morning I had to add up the previous day's sales that were recorded on little slips of paper that each department dropped on my desk before leaving at closing time. I had to add them with everyone eagerly awaiting the results. Lots of pressure first thing in the morning.

Another of my duties was to make the plane and hotel reservations for the buyers from each store to go to Italy, California and anywhere else they could find the best goods for the store. Each city had their own buyers that bought only for their stores so merchandise was not the same in every city.

My boss took care of any unusual returns that could not be handled in the departments. I remember a beautiful set of china being returned that they figured was about 50 years old because the gilt edging began to wear off, we cheerfully returned the money for that and many other items no store would ever take back today.

1953 Sheboygan Centennial Parade, photos taken from H. C. Prange store by Kathleen Bub Walker.

I loved learning about the behind the scenes things customers never see like the hidden offices and storage areas, the fact that the ding, ding, ding, you heard overhead was the operator paging someone, all the department and executives had their own bell code.

For many of us our first credit card was a Prange charge-a-plate. This was a metal charge card that came in a small paper envelope.

Besides shopping, from bargain basement to the exclusive Crystal Room eating at Prange's was always a treat especially the Shore Room with its blue leather booths that later became the Terrace Room.

I feel so blessed to have so many wonderful memories of this special store. For anyone who has had the Prange shopping experience shopping has never been the same.

Lynnette Hyink, Sheboygan, Wisconsin

I personally worked at Prange's in different departments such as Men's Clothing on first floor, the beauty salon on the fourth floor as a receptionist and a teller in the office on fourth floor between college and our marriage.

My mother, Arleen Hochwitz, was there for many years as the artist who drew the pictures for Prange's advertisements in the papers. She also ran the teen board, put on the bridal shows, back to school shows, and was in charge of the Christmas Children's Only shop in the basement at Christmas.

In the back of the store at the exit was a drive through for picking up lay-a-ways and various merchandise. This center was called Will-Call.

Before escalators were put in , there was a pretty marble stairway going down to the basement where the nice Shoreroom Restaurant was with large glass doors to enter and exit. When the basement shopping went more to a Prange-Way type, the restaurant went up to the second floor and was called the Terrace Room.

There were live mannequins or models placed around the clothing departments wearing clothing that was for sale.

On payday, Prange's would get quite a bit of its money back because we'd see things on our breaks and then go back and purchase them. We also got an employee discount.

Prange's tokens.

The Christmas Only Shop at Christmas time was for young children to go in and shop by themselves buying nice things inexpensively for people they wanted to give things to. This was located in the basement.

Top notch models came from Milwaukee to participate in some of the style shows. Teen board girls did modeling for the back-to-school shows with background music. My daughter, born in 1965, was a flower girl in one of the shows.

On the fourth floor was the advertising department, a book department, a furniture department and the Rogers Crocker studio and the offices.

In earlier years there was a stairway that went up there with two women in a glassed cubicle who ran the phone switchboard. Before the escalators went in there was an elevator that a woman ran for people and would ask what floor they wanted to go to.

Also, back then, we only had cash registers so you had to be good at math. There were no computers and no calculators.

On the first floor was a lunch counter with stools for customers or employees taking breaks. Also, on the fourth floor was a lounge room and rest room for employees.

Helen Mallmann, Sheboygan, Wisconsin

Prange's had a handkerchief department. A lady named Millie Mickenburg worked there. There was also a glove department which had a cushion on the counter, where you would rest your elbow as the clerk worked each finger down, then pulled the glove on the rest of the way.

There was also a hosiery department where the clerk, in order to show the color of the stockings, would make a fist and put it into the stocking and pull tight.

Book department located on the north wall of the store. A friend bought the Bobsy Twin series of books and an unhappy Clerk said she should be reading different books.

Some time in the 1950s I recall seeing a big man eating at the lunch counter. He was there with his daughter dressed all in pink. At times he carried her in his arms. This was unusual to have a father babysitting in the 1950s.

I remember there being a picture of Jesus framed and being sold in the grocery department.

The elevator operator turned a handle to operate the elevator.

One Christmas I took my five-year old niece to see the holiday windows. We took pictures and when we got them back there was a great image of Trinity Lutheran's steeple in the photo.

Connie Kuether, Howards Grove, Wisconsin

Albert (Al) Hierseman, my father, started working at the H.C. Prange Company in the printing department in April of 1923 at the age of 19. From there he went to the advertising department as a layout man, where he won many honors and awards in nationwide sportswear advertising and promotional contests for television and radio. He received gifts from some of those companies. One prize was the first television we had in our home, a Magnavox. Al was later promoted to advertising manager and in 1952 became advertising chief. He died in January 1956.

Claire Hierseman, my mother, worked part-time for three years in the shoe department before her husband, Al, died. In 1957 she was asked to return to work full-time. She began in the shoe department, but soon was transferred to the girdle and bra department where she eventually became the buyer for that department. Claire finished her career as the supervisor of the entire first floor, retiring in 1975 after eighteen years of service.

E.C. Hoyer, my uncle and my father's half-brother, started working at Prange's as a young man. He was a grocery delivery boy. My uncle told many stories of farmers bringing in their eggs, fruit and vegetable. In return they were given "due bills" with which they could buy merchandise in the store. He told about delivering groceries to homes along the shore of Lake Michigan, and about how that shoreline has changed as the water and erosion took away more and more of the shore. E.C. worked his way up from delivery boy to vice president of the H.C. Prange Company. He retired in 1968 after working there for forty-eight years.

Betsy Jones Michael, Sheboygan, Wisconsin

From an April 19, 1984 *Sheboygan Press* article

Nearly twenty years ago my husband came to San Francisco to ask me to marry him. He seemed to think he needed to talk me into it. As an inducement to come to this small town he mentioned we have the most marvelous department store. "A department store," I laughed aloud. A department store is a department store, I thought.

"No. Truly. It's unique," he said. "For instance, the Shoe Department. Any day you can walk through and see a lot of the older people in town. They come in to sit down. They're not there to buy shoes necessarily, but just to sit in out of the cold or get warm, or talk to their cronies, or just watch everybody go by." A town square, I thought, a Mexican Zocalo, the meeting place.

"You can get anything at Prange's," he said, "and if you don't like it, you can take it back."

"Of course, I always take things back, if they don't fit or don't work."

"No, this is different; you have to like it."

"Don't people take advantage of that?"

"I suppose so, but it probably evens out. Most people don't abuse things like that."

. . . "And the bakery," he went on, "when you walk downtown in the morning you can smell the hard rolls baking and Torke's coffee roasting. Everyone knows everyone else; the clerk's been there for years and knows what you like."

"Or don't like."

"Sure. I can call if I'm going to send one of the kids in for something and alert them and ask for their help. It's handy in my situation."

"In any situation?"

"Yes. I ordered a book the other day and they didn't have it. But they got it right away. Then they called to ask whether I'll pick it up in Will Call or wanted it delivered.

"They treat everyone that way?"

"Yes, it's their policy."

. . . It's special treatment, true, but not preferential; everyone has a Prange tale or two. Those extra services and personal touches were what put Prange's in a high class of its own. Much of that cannot be duplicated nor replaced; that kind of help from knowledgeable personnel is irreplaceable.

Anonymous

What was Prange's like in the 1930s? The store was comprised of 80% men and 20% women. The full-time employees worked six days a week, earning 25 cents per hour. Each customer was individually attended. Sales checks were written and sent to the Cash Office for change– by pneumatic tubes (The pneumatic tubes were removed in the 1950s). There were only two large sales each year, Demonstration Sale and Anniversary Sale in October. The windows provided both light and summer air movement – no air conditioning.

Jan Hildebrand, Sheboygan Falls, WI from a July 1992, *Sheboygan Press* article
Only memories will remain 'down by Prange's'

. . . Friday nights were traditional shopping nights and the Prange's corner was crowded until after the 9 p.m. closing. Husbands waited for their wives in the shoe department taking advantage of the center of the store location and comfortable seats. The lunch counter was a favorite of teenagers drinking soda and eating French fries. Mom could lunch with friends at the fourth floor restaurant and everyone started their Christmas shopping during the anniversary sale in October.

. . . Another more practical tradition was the E.O.M. (end of month) sales. These occurred the last Wednesday of each month when stock was discounted for sale. Huge crowds waited to get in at 9a.m.

. . . Prange's will be no more. Other companies have closed their doors, but Prange's was the heart and soul of Sheboygan. Sheboygan without Prange's is like a brat without the hard roll, Christmas without Santa and the riverfront without the river. Sheboygan will weather the loss, but the memories will linger.

John Schultz,

May Day Event– 1926 Prange Review magazine– May Day Queen is Marie Grunewald, mother of John Schultz. She was 23 years old at the time, born February 23, 1903.

Prange's Drapery department workroom
1970
Back right, Annette Reif

Pam Sundell, Kiel, Wisconsin

I grew up with Prange's. I shopped with my mother, aunts and grandma when I was little. I sat on Santa's lap in the 1940s to tell him my wishes. And every year after Thanksgiving I waited with eager anticipation for those animated Christmas windows to be revealed. I took the bus to Prange's with my friends when I was older. There is no floor I didn't visit; restaurants, grocery store, toys, clothes, furniture, books, caramel corn, candy, bakery and everything in between. Our big box store! It had everything. My wedding and bridesmaids' dresses were from Prange's as well as my china pattern. My husband went to look at the train layouts when he was a boy. We got our first Christmas lights, ornaments and manger upstairs at the after-Christmas sale the winter before we got married. We still use that star on top of our tree. When our children came along we took them to see Santa and view those Christmas windows, too. Prange's was very much a part of my life for many years and four generations. We miss Prange's! P.S. It's great to see those window displays again at the museum each year.

Vernon Jaberg, Elkhart Lake, Wisconsin

When I was a student at Mission House College (1940-1946) I worked weekends at Prange's in the men's department during the school year and for Chicago Northwestern Railroad during the summer.

Milford Boll was the purchaser for the Men's Department at the time. He traveled to New York on a regular basis to get the latest in fashion. Albert Korthels was the head of the Boys and Men's' department. We sold suits, overcoats, trousers and supplied graduation robes for students. Ernst Johnson and Herb Konsky were the credit checkers at the time.

One of my favorite memories was the day we sold twenty-three suits. The only two types of suits available at the time were Bankers Gray for $22 and Business Stripe for $25. It was during World War II and the government had just passed a new ordinance which required lapels to be cut narrow and pants to have no cuffs in order to save material. The styles changed drastically and as a result men needed new suits. The head tailor at the time was Al Claymeier, a German immigrant who editorialized on a regular basis—Cuffs on! Cuffs off! Cuffs on! Cuffs Off! Each suit was boxed for the customer by the girls in the wrapping room.

Prange's was good to students. There was always a group of kids from Mission House who washed lights and wiped down pipes in order to keep Prange's looking its best. While there, the ever-hungry students could eat anything they wanted.

I also remember selling suits to two very, very tall basketball players who were in town playing against the Redskins.

Like many others, I have very fond memories of working at Prange's.

Barbara Rickmeyer, Sheboygan, Wisconsin

My first job was at Prange's in the gift wrap department which also did wrapping for shipping and delivery. Once, after doing an overseas packing job, the German lady who was shipping things home, left a $20.00 tip. This was in 1945 and I made 55 cents per hour. I later worked as a cashier and made change. (That $20 would be $250 today.)

We loved to go to Prange's. We have such nice memories of the bakery department and the caramel corn balls available all year around.

Sandra Engelman Van Erem, Sheboygan, Wisconsin

Here we go on a sentimental journey. When I hear the name Prange's, a lot comes to mind. I spent a great deal of time on Eighth Street between the ages of twelve and seventeen (1965-1970). We would hang around Eighth Street because that was the hip place to hang out. Sometimes we would go to the Sheboygan Theater to see a movie or we would go to "Jupiter" across the street from Prange's for soda or to Hills for cheap nylons. But, Prange's was the best. We would ride the escalators. Then we would go downstairs and get 45rpm records for 88 cents each. I still have all of mine. They had the latest, up-to-date records. Then we would go and get a hot dog and some candy or bakery at the counters. The biggest treat was the homemade caramel corn. Oh, my mouth is watering. Prange's was the best. Many times we would have to wait until a new batch was made. Of course, we would watch carefully and hurry to get the fresh, warm caramel corn. I doesn't get better than that.

Many times I remember going to Prange's with mom, aunt and grandma and eating lunch in the upstairs restaurant. I think it was on the second floor. We had many good lunches up there. We would also stand and watch the sailors come in on Friday nights. They would walk from the naval station after arriving on the 880. It was always warm in the front entrance even though the doors were open.

Prange's was the place to go in the 1960s and 1970s. I will never forget the Prange's good times.

Karl J. Vercouteren, The Dalles, Oregon

Julius Ochs, my grandfather, owned two acres at the corner of 23rd Street and Erie Avenue. In the 1940s about half of the property was a truck garden. I remember accompanying grandpa on Saturdays when he sold produce at Prange's Farmers' Market. It was held Saturdays and perhaps other days in a large building across Wisconsin Avenue from the grocery entrance to the main store. The building was probably a former garage or even a stable. (It was the Prange livery– first housing horses, then cars.) Big garage doors were rolled up or folded back on either end to turn it into a large, open-air space.

Thanksgiving evening in the 1940s was a wondrous event. This was when the mechanical Christmas display was unveiled in the big windows at the corner of Eighth Street and Wisconsin Avenue. There was always a big crowd jostling for a look. The weather was usually frosty and sometimes snowy. You knew the Christmas season arrived when Schuster's Department Store in Milwaukee held its Santa

Claus parade and when the Prange's windows went on display.

Back in the 1940s people didn't pay their bills via mail or credit card. Mother would take my brothers and me on a route that began at Citizens Bank to withdraw money and pay the Christmas Club installment. Then we'd ride up the elevator in our town's one and only skyscraper, the Security Bank building to pay the monthly Metropolitan Life premium. Aunt Elsie Fasse worked at Dr. Doyle's dental office on the second floor and Edie, the elevator operator, was her friend. This was always a place to stop and visit. Then we would crisscross downtown, stopping at various stores to settle up the month's charges or to put money down on "lay-away" merchandise. Those excursions always took us to the mysterious fourth floor of Prange's. Mysterious, in that the escalators connected the basement, main, second and third floors, which were wide open, well-lit sales floors. The fourth floor, however, consisted of dark and narrow hallways leading to offices including the one where we paid our bill. The Rogers Crocker Photography Studio was on that floor, where some of us would go for graduation photos many years later. The other doors were sometimes left open and we could get a glimpse of store officialdom, occasionally H.C. Prange himself. And if we were really lucky, the door would be open to a room filled with naked mannequins!

One time in the mid-1950s Sheboygan suffered a snow storm so severe that the superintendent closed the public schools. But, we high-schoolers braved the blizzard to engage in one of our favorite social activities - riding the escalators at Prange's. In fact, enough kids crowded that store that there were complaints.

My major memories of the old Prange store go back to college days. I began my freshman year at Lakeland College in the fall of 1957. Money was in short supply even though tuition was ridiculously low by current standards and I saved even more by living at home and commuting that first year. My fellow commuter, old scouting buddy and soon-to-be fraternity brother, Eric Torrison, told me about a job he was starting, one that fit our schedule. It wasn't big money, but it would help. It was working part-time on the after-hours clean-up crew at Prange's.

So I applied and was hired. The first stop was Mr. Maier's office. He was the boss of building maintenance. Mr. M. had a standard lecture for new hires, especially young ones. "This is not clean-up to the standard your mother uses when she cleans the kitchen, " he told us. We were to do a quick job of making the store presentable for the next day. Then every once-in-a-while there would be a more thorough cleaning project.

We prepared to swing into action when the store closed at 5:30 p.m. Bernie was foreman of the night crew. He issued us our badge of office: a putty knife to carry in our back pocket for scraping gum off the terrazzo or vinyl tile floors. Bernie introduced us to our assignments and showed us where brooms and mops and vacuum cleaners were stored, how to find our way around the maze of back rooms and passageways that the public never saw, where the light switches were– lots to remember, but all neatly broken down into manageable tasks.

We set off with gusto, finishing our first jobs in half the time Bernie said it would take. We reported back for the next assignments and instead of being commended for our efficiency, we received Bernie's standard lecture for new hires, especially young ones, "Take your time and do the job in the time allotted for it. The rest of the crew are much older than you, and they'll resent it if you finish way ahead of them."

It was good advice. Others on the crew were much older, some pushing retirement or beyond. They included my Uncle John Otte, a quiet, short man well along in years. Some of the men befriended us novices and gave us hints about doing various jobs. Others hardly spoke to us and simply went about their tasks each night.

There were low points and high points in our evening's rounds. Cleaning the public restrooms was never much fun. If messes were left behind, that's where we would find them. When there was a major clean-up, it entailed wrestling the heavy duty rotating scrubbing machines that threatened to whirl out of control.

The bakery invited us in with pleasant smells, but that was where I encountered my first roaches, probably imported from warmer climes on or in corrugated boxes. (Years later I lived in the South and a neighbor up from the hills said, "T'aint a shame to HAVE roaches, but hit's a shame if you don't FIGHT 'em.) Scraping up the grease that had splattered out of the doughnut vat and fed those creatures that scurried away when we turned on the lights was almost enough to put me off Prange's delicious bakery products forever.

OSHA would have frowned upon the way we cleaned the escalators. We rode them up and down frantically scrubbing fingerprints off the aluminum walls, all the while hoping wash rags or clothing wouldn't catch in the machinery. The handrails were easier. We stood in one place with a sponge in each hand as the rubber rails slid by.

Fun jobs were cleaning the toy department, housewares and the hardware department. There we could speed up the sweeping or mopping and spend the time we saved checking out the newest gadgets. Likewise, with the appliance department that was in a building across the alley. Nobody came around to check up on us, so we did our job quickly and then could flip on one of the floor model demonstration TVs and grab a five-minute break. We could explore the mysterious nooks and crannies that the public never saw and the mysteries—to the men—of the lingerie department.

The half-time schedule gave us enough pay to make the job worthwhile, while the hours were short enough to give us time for college-level homework and reading assignments. The pay was even better, but the job was a lot worse when it morphed from part-time to full-time. That happened as we approached Christmas. Not only was the store dirtier than ever, given large crowds that often tracked in sand, salt and slush. But, also the hours changed. We were asked to work a nine to five shift — that is a 9 p.m. to 5 a.m. shift when the store was closed. These were the wee hours of the morning and it was near the end of the college term. We let others in the carpool drive after we grabbed an hour or two of sleep. I believe napping on the way to and from Lakeland and dozing in class was the only way we made it through the weeks from Thanksgiving to Christmas.

I worked at Prange's through the school year of 1957-1958 and then quit to return to my favorite summer job at Camp Rokilio. After that I lived on campus and found part-time jobs at Lakeland. But, I knew the ropes of the night cleaning crew at Prange's and filled in holidays and a few other short-time stints as I continued my college career.

There are other Prange Store memories—like some of the people who worked there. There was Herb Ruehl, the always-dapper "floor walker." He was stationed in the main aisle that led from the Eighth Street entrance. He would greet people, direct them to the store's many departments and cast a disapproving eye on teenagers whose only reason for being in Prange's was to ride the escalators. There was my old Sunday school teacher, Harvey Rackow, who worked the grocery parking lot and its entrance in all kinds of weather, helping Sheboygan's matrons load their groceries into their cars. There was also my cousin, Florence Jensema, who tried to fix me up with a redhead who worked with her in the Prange's basement.

Then there was the time I tried to sell an ad in the college newspaper to an advertising manager in one of those fourth floor cubbys. Prange's was good for a little "compliments of" ad in Lakeland's annual, but I had visions of a large display ad in the newspaper. After all, it was in Prange's interest to turn college students into customers. The gentleman turned me down flat, saying that Prange's had doled out all their charitable donations for the year! The experience taught me that sales was not my long suit. I became an ordained minister, a career that did involve "sales" to a certain degree. But, it also entailed a whole lot of building maintenance, sometimes swinging a mop, and often cleaning up other people's messes - skills that I honed at an early age at the old H.C. Prange store.

Mary Bowser Deeley, Sheboygan Falls, Wisconsin - age 95
Prange's was the place to shop many, many years ago. This was time when people would bring their eggs and whatever to the store and turn them in for credit in the store. I still hear the phrase, "Down by Prange's" ringing in my ears.

Women very seldom drove in the early quarter of the 20th century, so husbands brought their wives in for shopping. The Prange store had benches beside the store where men would sit and wait while their wives were in the store as shopping was something that wives usually took care of.

One shopping day, my father, John Bowser, was sitting on a bench visiting with friends, waiting for my mother Matie Bowser to finish her shopping, when a woman walked out of the store carrying her baby. She walked toward the corner, then paused and turned back. She looked at the men sitting on then bench, then, choosing Dad, walked up to him and asked if he would hold her baby as she had forgotten something and needed to run back into the store for it.

Another time, another place. Dad held the baby and the woman came back in a few minutes with her purchase and reclaimed him. No child welfare agents were called, and no child disappeared.

Nancy Klein, Glenbeulah, Wisconsin

Prange's! What a store! All my memories of Prange's are wonderful. It was simply the best store in the world. On Saturdays, my best friend and I would hop on the number seven bus toward downtown. The highlight of the day was stopping at Prange's whether we bought anything or just spent the day looking. There was so much to see. Silver charms for $2.00. Shampoo in the notions department. You name it, Prange's had it.

My fondest memory is of my sister and I going to Prange's with our mom to pick our patterns and fabrics for clothes she would make for us. In those days, Prange's had no petites department, and most of the clothes were too large for us, so our mom would sew us dresses, suits and pants, and knit us sweaters. We would take the escalator to the second floor, and step off into a world of countless fabrics, trim, yarns and patterns to choose from. It was better than buying clothes off the rack, because we could design our own. Spectacular! To this day, I still design and sew much of my own clothing, thanks to my mom and Prange's.

Lorrie Wilson, Sheboygan Falls, Wisconsin

Prange's was a family. My husband, Jerry Wilson, injured himself while working at Prange's. He was told to put his leg up for two weeks, but we were scheduled to move across town that same week. We tried to wrangle as many family members and friends with station wagons as we could. Moments before the moving was to start, the Prange's truck and about eight men from the warehouse showed up and moved the us. They took no payment

Prange's memorabilia from Lorrie and Jerry Wilson's collection. At upper right is a Prange's 22nd anniversary plate—1887 to 1909. At right is a Prange's key ring. Below left is an H.C. Prange shoe horn and at lower right is an H.C. Prange Company commemorative spoon.

Barbara Fischer, Milwaukee, Wisconsin

North Eighth Street in Sheboygan was synonymous with the H.C. Prange Company during the 1950s and 1960s. Department stores like Hills, J.C. Penney Company and Montgomery Ward lined Eighth Street along with Mullen's Appliance, Woolworth's, Kresge's, Nobil Shoes, Three Sisters and others. Friday nights kids cruised Eighth Street honking horns, squealing tires and waving to friends.

Cars cruising Eighth Street were visible from just inside Prange's. The non-existent front entrance were replaced by fans blasting heat from the ceiling and floor. No matter what time of year you walked into the front entrance without having to manage a door.

Beyond the front entrance, the first area to greet the customer was the cosmetic counter. This announced the promise of beautiful things inside. This is where I worked. At sixteen this was my dream job. I remember running home from the bus stop to tell my mother my good fortune to get a job at Prange's. This was so thrilling.

My boss was Rena Parks, along with Ruth Voight, Janie DePagter, Gail Dawson and others we manned the department. I worked Friday evenings and all day Saturday. During Christmas holidays we sold lots of gift fragrance sets like Tabu, Blue Grass, Intimate and Shalimar. On Christmas Eve the store closed at 4:30pm. Mr. Prange, just before closing, would go through the store and shake every clerk's hand and with them Merry Christmas. My next brush with celebrity was in 1966.

Sheboygan's runner-up to Miss America, Mary Alice Fox, came into the store. She came through the front entrance past the cosmetic counter and disappeared. I didn't really get a glimpse of her because she was looking toward the men's department. Word spread quickly among the clerks she had been in their department. Everyone tried to be so nonchalant about her being there. On her way out she stopped in the cosmetics department and talked with the clerk stationed as a look-out behind the counter on the main aisle.

Mary Alice was stunning and the image of what every young girl believed Miss America should be. Not only was she beautiful, but she seemed so poised and unhurried. She left as she arrived, through the front entrance without fanfare or entourage.

Footnote: When former employees meet, the conversation about Prange's simply continues as if the store had never closed. It was a wonderful work-life at Prange's and a delight for a young girl.

Lou Eva Horneck Schmahl, Elkhart Lake, Wisconsin

Going to Sheboygan with my parents (we lived about twenty miles from there) to take eggs to Prange's in exchange for groceries was always an exciting time for me. It also meant going to a few other stores, but Prange's was our special store.

I remember going up the escalator, going into the bargain basement and eating at the restaurant in Prange's. My favorite item on the menu was always the German potato salad and wieners.

I remember my mother giving me permission to pick out two comic books to buy while she shopped nearby. Then we'd go up the escalator and pay some money for what we owed from the time before. Times were hard then. When we were ready to go home, we'd go upstairs from the main floor to the restrooms and from there we'd sit in a balcony-type room where we could see other people shopping and watch for my dad to come in from the street entrance to pick us up. But, first he'd always buy his favorite candy, chocolate peanut clusters. They became my favorite, too.

As we left we'd go into the back room where we and other shoppers had their grocery boxes ready to pick-up and take to the car in the parking lot.

Christmas was always special to my brother and I. Those animated show windows at Prange's were fun to see. We went close to the area inside the store to watch Santa talk to other children saying what they wanted for Christmas, but we never stood in line.

It was accepted by me that on previous trips to Prange's without us that our parents had told Santa what we wanted. I could picture my mom standing in line with other children waiting to talk to him.

One year my brother and I came across some items of interest in their bedroom closet shelf. Later it ended up under the Christmas tree. That was the end of our special gifts from the man in the red suit who always would come into our locked living room the day before Christmas, putting gifts under the tree.

In 1953 I bought my mother two nine-inch pink ceramic parrots for one dollar each. I still have them and later I bought my first book of Laura Ingalls Wilder Little House series in the book department.

When I became engaged to be married, wedding plans slowly formed in my mind. The bridal department at Prange's featured a dress to my liking. It was a floor-length gown of satin, lace and net, styled with a Peter Pan collar. The cost was $99.00 ($813 today). My head veil was $23.00 ($189.00 today). Shoes for $5.00 ($41 today). That seemed expensive for the time. My mother paid for the dress and I paid for the veil and shoes by doing housework and baby-sitting at the time for people in Ada and Rhine Center.

Joyce Braeger Krahn, Rhinelander, Wisconsin

Adeliah Dassow Braeger, my mother, completed Lutheran high school in Minnesota at the age of sixteen and following a year of teaching at Laurium in Michigan's upper peninsula copper country joined the faculty at a Lutheran school in Sheboygan. This was a prized position in 1928. She taught fifty third and fourth graders, but still had some free time, so she took an enjoyable job at Prange's over the Christmas vacation. When school officials found out, Adeliah was told in no uncertain terms that it wasn't proper for a parochial teacher to be clerking at a department store. She continued teaching at the school until the following June when she returned to Vesper where she clerked in her father's general store.

Audrey Ertl, St. Nazianz, Wisconsin

My grandparents had a farm on what was then the old 17 road just north of Erdman. Now the road is Dairyland Drive. They had cows, sheep, pigs, chickens, geese and horses to do the farm work. There was a garden and an apple orchard. The sheep, gray or black, were sheared for the wool. Then my grandmother washed it and after it was dry she carded it. Then she spun it into yarn. She died the yarn using beets for red. I'm not sure what she used for green. The yarn was used for knitting to make vests, sweaters, socks, gloves and mittens.

She never had any money of her own. But, Prange's' provided a way for her to get things she needed. Eggs, produce from the garden, apples from the orchard and even butchered chickens and geese were sold to Prange's for the all-important due bill. If you didn't have due bills you couldn't buy anything, so said my grandfather. Prange's sure had a monopoly.

The chickens and geese brought to Prange's only had the feathers removed. The feet and head, etc. remained intact. If someone wanted to buy poultry at Prange's it was first weighted. It cost extra to have the head, feet and innards removed. Things sure have improved at meat markets since that day.

Jim Schoerger, Houston, Texas

I grew up in Sheboygan and attended North High School — Class of 1955. One winter the temperatures dipped low and they closed the schools. That day, all the school kids headed to Prange's for a day of playing and riding the escalators. After that, the schools decided that if all the kids could go to Prange's, they could go to school. They didn't close the schools after that.

Pat Schoerger, Houston, Texas

In the early 1970s, I had the opportunity to work at Prange's during the Christmas holidays. I worked in the Men's Shirt Department located on the first floor. One day someone returned an unwrapped Prange's white dress shirt that had to be over twenty years old for a refund. There was no way to even guess what the shirt originally sold for, so being the kind of store that Prange's was, we just pulled a number out of the air and issued a refund.

Pat Resimius, Plymouth, Wisconsin

In the mid-1950s my Grandma Gannon would take us all to Prange's for our Easter outfits. My mom would drive because Grandma never had a license. The best part of the day was the hot dog and root beer at the Hot Dog Counter. Just thinking about it makes me smile.

Minnie VanWyk Veldman, Plymouth, Wisconsin

It was in late winter of 1945 that I looked in the local paper, and as I was unemployed at the time, was looking in the Help Wanted section. One ad drew my attention. It was from H.C. Prange Company looking for a baker's assistant in their Silver Edge Bakery.

I applied the next day and was hired immediately. Along with four other girls, Deloris, Bernice, Verna and Irene. We were kept busy six days each week icing cakes, sugaring donuts and placing these on delivery racks for Casey, the delivery man, to take down to the grocery department where the clerks placed them in the cases for sale.

It being war time there was rationing of sugar, shortening, flour and other commodities so there was a limit to how much the bakers could make each day. Needless to say, I enjoyed my time at the bakery very much. To this day I use some of their techniques in my own kitchen. It all came to an end in 1946 when my fiancée returned from the war in the Pacific and we were married and went to reside in Plymouth.

Doris Breitzman, left, and Helen Dionne, right

Doris Breitzman Sievers Towsley, Sheboygan, Wisconsin

I was a secretary in the Home Furnishing Division of Prange's for over twenty years and then worked part-time until 1971. They had a secretary on each floor starting with the basement. The basement was low priced merchandise, toys, tools, etc. The secretaries were: Joyce Metcher, basement; Arlene Verhage, first floor Men's Department; Florence Kohl, second floor and Doris Breitzman (me) on the third floor. The Executive Offices and accounting offices were on the fourth floor.

First floor had the Grocery Department at one end and then the shoes, men's wear, ladies apparel, hand bags, etc. The second floor was for bedding, women's apparel and hats. The third floor was for draperies, floor coverings, furniture, lamps, dishes, gifts, also, stoves and other appliances. Ray Daniels, Sr. was the Home Furnishings Director. Other department heads were: Willard Miller, furniture; Walter Glaeser, floor coverings; Eitel Meyer, lamps, dishes, records; and Curt Wedepohl was director of draperies. There was a wrapping stand on the third floor which was run by Jane Poppe. I was secretary on that floor.

Arlene Verhage, Secretary, First Floor Men's Dept. 1947

All of the departments were close knit and got together for any reason (picnics, anniversaries, etc.)

What I remember most is that on Friday nights all of the secretaries had to help out in the Main Office, also on the third floor. The reason was that all of the factories had pay day on Friday and the banks were not open so they came to Prange's to cash their checks. There were eight windows and the people would be lined up ten deep at each window to cash their checks. I remember having one elderly man wait at my window for a long time each Friday because he could not talk English and I could talk German to him.

Joyce Metcher Zeineman, Secretary Basement

Front row: Dorothy Radtke, Edna Sarau, Doris Breitzman, Edithe Sievers at Edna's house.
Back row: Unknown.
Prange's employees having fun together in 1943.

Mr. and Mrs. Walter Glaeser's anniversary party in 1944. All of the employees from the third floor attended.

Edna Sarau, sales person in Draperies. Image taken in June of 1949.

Doris Breitzman at left, Meta Verhage, center, and unknown at right. At Edna Sarau's house.

There wasn't any overtime for all the additional hours. It just went with the job. When I first started in 1941 I earned $15.00 per week, $60.00 per month. You could buy a lot with that money in those days.

Also on Friday nights each secretary had to take turns working in the War Bonds Booth during World War II. It was on the first floor near the Shoe Department.

> **Write Your Name on a Bomb for Japan**
> 1943
>
> For three days in April of 1943 Prange's made a real push to sell record numbers of war bonds. Every purchaser had the opportunity to write his or her name on a 500 pound bomb aimed for Japan.
>
> Three 500 lb. bombs, each nearly five feet tall, with fins manufactured by Sheboygan's own Garton Toy Company, stood next to the bond booth, ready for signing.

At left: WWII Bond and Stamp Booth at Prange's. Taken on December 4, 1942.

Roland Schomberg, Howards Grove, Wisconsin
From a March 7, 1986 *Sheboygan Press* article

As a small boy, a trip to Sheboygan in the late 1920s generally triggered mixed emotions for me. Because of the rarity of the occasion and the fact that I had a great fear of getting lost in "the big city," the announcement that I would be accompanying my parents to town on a shopping trip wasn't necessarily greeted with unbounded enthusiasm.

I guess my greatest concern was the terror I experienced riding the four-story H.C. Prange Co. elevator My mother's hands must have turned knuckle-white as I hung on to them for dear life from the time the elevator attendant flipped the starting switch until he announced the number of the floor or our destination. Fortunately we were never trapped between floors.

. . . The entrance to Prange's at this location was a favorite gathering place as the farmers waited for their "due bill" or merely exchanged small talk and met old friends. The store furnished numerous benches which were positioned on the sidewalk for the convenience of their customers, although it was a favorite haunt of also for non-buyers who often participated in the open forums conducted there.

This particular spot proved to be a big attraction for me also, since rows and rows of large, luscious oranges arranged on a slant in pyramid fashion were displayed in the large store windows on either side of the store entrance. In our family, bananas and oranges were delicacies that were reserved for special occasions like Christmas or Easter and my mouth would water as I pressed my nose against the cold plate glass window and drank in the whole scene.

. . . I had a problem with the mannequins, finding it hard to keep from associating them with funeral parlors and wondering if they had been alive at one time.

. . . Another area in the store that fascinated me was the shoe department. This was the designated stop for us to reassemble for the long trip home since there were dozens of comfortable seats where the first to arrive could relax and wait for the stragglers. The chairs were intended to be used in the fitting of shoes, though at times it was not readily apparent that this was the case. The majority of my shoes were purchased here if for no other reason than for the thrill we experienced from sliding our feet into the X-ray machine in the center of the department. The machine was used extensively to assure the customers of properly fitting footwear. In no other place in the county could one look through one's shoes and watch the toe bones flexing.

No sojourn to the city would have been complete without a visit to the spacious Prange basement. Though it was accessible by elevator, I preferred to take the wide, solid stairway to the lower level. Once downstairs, a life-size model dapple-gray horse in the farm department in the east end of the floor was the big attraction for me.

Ron Klunk and Jerry Wilson, Sheboygan and Sheboygan Falls, Wisconsin
Prange's fur department was once robbed in broad daylight during the lunch hour.

The artwork for H.C. Prange was done by Art Lensink. His grandson now owns Art's Display at the Riverfront.

C. Reiss Coal once delivered oil to H.C. Prange but pumped it into the wrong pipe. The basement ended up with about 1" of oil on the floor. All the counters had to have the bottoms cut and replaced to get rid of the oil stains and smell.

The first restaurant, the Shore Room, at Prange's was located in the basement until about 1960.

People would come to Prange's and spend the entire day at the store.

Every Christmas Eve the staff sang carols and even the management would join in. H. Carl Prange wished each employee a Merry Christmas.

Each year on the night before the Anniversary Sale in October when the store was closed skits to motivate the staff were put on by the employees. (Photo at right)

The corporate offices of H.C. Prange were Spartan by all accounts. The only thing that was unusual was that the Public Relations employee had an elevated desk.

Shoplifters were detained and talked to by management. In the 1960s a professional police presence was hired by the store. Women carried see-through shopping bags. Employees were not allowed to check themselves out. They needed to have another associate take care of the transaction.

Periodically, celebrities were engaged to help promote the company or various products. Florence Henderson represented the company from 1984-1985. She appeared at one of the company's big fashion shows. Jesse White, the Maytag repairman, was also engaged to increase sales. Pat O'Brien sold his book and appeared at the store.

The Prange Company's extraordinary charity work was done quietly. It went unrecognized as planned.

Prange's delivery service was second to none. It was good for something a small as a 5 ¢ greeting card.

The semi-annual White Sale was initiated for the multiple houses of ill repute in Sheboygan. The madams needed to restock their businesses and wanted the best from Prange's. They expected good prices and purchased in large quantities.

Maytag repairman, Jesse White and Ron Klunk

When the store collapsed and had to close and then be cleared out, Pinkerton Services boxed and removed the merchandise.

The Lay-Away Department was so large it required an entire warehouse. The space used was the old Lincoln Ford Garage in downtown Sheboygan.

Stan Gehr was Santa Claus and his wife was Mrs. Claus. Remember Bruce the Talking Spruce?

Rogers Crocker had his photography studio in the store.

Leroy Ottensmann, Sheboygan, Wisconsin
Mildred Mayr Kramer, Leroy's mother-in-law, played piano in the Music Department at Prange's. Her job was to play requested music. She was also a live model downstairs in the store.

Besides playing at Prange's, Mildred played piano for the silent movies at the Lincoln Theater, once located at 12th Street and Lincoln Avenue.

Bernie Markevitch, Sheboygan, Wisconsin
From a July 1990 special to *The Press*
Hot Dogs signaled the most memorable occasions
My grandmother like to serve wieners for Sunday supper with baked beans and German potato salad plus a whole lot of other food including the Jell-O she always forgot to serve with the always elaborate Sunday dinner we had consumed at noon. . .

Santa, Stan Gehr, sits at his post at Prange's North Pole.

For me, life's great occasions seemed to be marked with the serving of hot dogs. We got them at the Safety Patrol Christmas party, the school picnic and all the really good birthday parties.

When my family moved here in the mid-50s, one of the great discoveries was Prange's hot dog counter. I loved those hot dogs instantly. . .

While a student at Central High, I usually went home for lunch except for the really cold days in the winter. Then Mother would give me a quarter to get hot lunch in the school cafeteria. But those twenty-five cents bought two hot dogs "with the works, please," and a frosty mug of root beer.

I graduated without ever eating in the school cafeteria.

In those good old days when Eisenhower was president and all a teenager had to worry about was the bomb and acne, the hot dog stand at Prange's was just off the main aisle, between the grocery and the lunch counter. It wasn't very large and it wasn't a place to linger.

Cora a tiny little gray-haired lady, ran that stand with an iron hand. I was sure she was a retired

Gestapo agent. Anyone caught rapping their quarter on the countertop immediately lost his turn in the lineup and got a withering glance that said plenty.

Impatience was not allowed and talking back or impertinence only made it worse. . .

In all the upheaval of the mid-60s came upheaval on the home front as well. Prange's remodeled the whole store, inside and out.

They moved everything around including the hot dog stand. They shoved it into a larger space in the corner and added things to the menu, but hot dogs were the only thing I ever ordered there. They added a number machine and Cora was still there (a thread of continuity ever vigilant for those coin rappers). A quarter bought the root beer now and the hot dogs were 2 for 75 cents.

Nettie Meulbroek,
The caramel corn lady at H.C. Prange's.

The hot dog stand vanished in the great fire. . . .

Post Script — There are so many memories associated with that store and its piece in the story of Sheboygan retailing. I felt, growing up, why go elsewhere — we love it here . . . And it wasn't until the old store was gone did I ever realize how much we lost. Even though there was a new store what we'd lost was significant.

Lorrie and Jerry Wilson, Sheboygan Falls, Wisconsin

Prange's once had a manager who put his desk on a platform so he would always be looking down at you.

Toyland was first located on the fourth floor in the furniture section and there were two huge toy soldiers made of cardboard, covered in felt standing guard at the entrance.

The hot dog roller from the hot dog counter at Prange's is today at B & B Ford in Sheboygan Falls.

Gary Strochein got his hand stuck in the escalator about 1953.

Prange's Food Stamp and Good Luck tokens,
Scott Lewandoske collection

Jennifer Intravaia Tyskiewicz, New Berlin, **Charles Intravaia and James Intravaia**

The three of us grew up in Sheboygan during the 1940's through 1960's. Our mom, Jennie E. Intravaia, worked at Prange's Department Store from the late 1950's until 1977. She put her excellent skills as a seamstress to work, first in the Ladies Alteration Room, and then, as Manager of the Drapery Workroom. We've put together some memories of Prange's from our childhood and from Mom's workdays there.

The Prange's of our childhood was the place to go to meet your friends, much like today's malls, but all in one building. We didn't do much "buying," of course, but mostly just looked around, had a bite to eat, or listened to music in the Record Department. Kresge's Dime Store was across the street to the north at the time, and Hills Department Store was across 8th Street to the west. Hills was often referred to by adults as the "dry goods store," and was not nearly as interesting to kids as Prange's was!

Prange's was a "full-service" department store back in those days. There was a wonderful bakery that, we somehow found out, housed its' ovens and baking area underground, going south in the direction of the old Playdium Bowling Alley and the Wisconsin Theater. This bakery produced rum-flavored cupcakes and poppy seed cake that stand out in our memories as being special treats that Mom would occasionally bring home.

There was a deli area and a grocery area, and Prange's even delivered groceries to your door in those days. As children, we were drawn to the 10-cent hot dog counter for a very reasonable deal. We were also attracted to the Shoe Department, for the sole purpose of using the X-Ray machine that revealed our skeletal foot! Those machines were taken out of stores eventually, when it was found that overexposure to needless x-rays was not a good thing for the body!

A trip to Prange's always included a visit to the Record Department, which for much of our childhood, was located in the basement, next to the elevators. At one time, there were even booths that you could take a record into to listen to, presumably to make a decision as to if you wanted to purchase it. That was extreme trust on the part of Prange management in those days, as it certainly could have resulted in plenty of scratched records in not-very-careful hands. In the early 1960's, we recall that Bart Starr, legendary Packers quarterback, made an appearance to sign autographs in the Record Department.

The basement area also included, for a time, the "bargain area," a true "bargain basement," so to speak, that may have been called "Prangeway," and was the beginnings of the Prangeway Store that eventually moved to Kohler Memorial Drive.

Mom's Ladies Alteration Room and Drapery Workroom were located in rooms "behind the scenes." Most customers would never know that there was a small group of very dedicated women working diligently behind the store backdrops. Mom used to laugh about the time when they first piped music into the store for the shopping enjoyment of customers. The poor ladies in the Ladies Alteration Room would somehow only hear the bass part of the music back behind-the-scenes, always leaving them wondering as to what song was playing!

We were sorry to hear, at the time, of the eventual plans to close Prange's, because the more stream-lined store that took its place didn't have the character and services once offered under one roof.

Helen Hanson, Lombard, Illinois

I wanted you to know how much I enjoyed your article on Prange's. As a 91 year old who lived in Sheboygan until I graduated from Central High School in 1938, I can remember many, many trips to Prange's with my Mother--to all floors and all departments. She also told of my getting lost in Prange's basement when I was about 3 or 4 years old. My mother stopped to talk to Eitel Meyer, who I believe was a salesman on the basement floor at the time and a family friend, and I became impatient and wandered off to explore other aisles--suddenly crying and screaming because I couldn't find my way back. (We think a very common happening in Prange's. I'm sure they were well equipped to find lost parents.)

Chris Roenitz, Sheboygan, Wisconsin

"My mother and I went to pick up my birthday cake at Prange's. In those days, there were no seat belts and big back seats. So I was standing up and leaning over the front seat (looking at the cake we had just retrieved). My mother stopped abruptly and I (went over the seat and) landed in the cake. I did not cry. I just stood there in horror. My mother turned the car around. No scold-ing because she knew it was an accident. She bumped into Carl Prange in the store and told him what had happened. He told us to come back in two hours. They would make a new birthday cake. Service hey!"

H. C. Prange Favorites

Prange's Sour Cream Muffins

1/2 cup butter
1 cup sugar
2 eggs
1 tsp. vanilla
1 cup sour cream
2 cups flour
1 tsp. baking powder
1 tsp. baking soda
1/4 tsp. salt
1/4 tsp. mace
Cinnamon and sugar mixture

Cream butter and sugar until fluffy. Add eggs, one at a time. Mix in vanilla. Combine flour, baking powder, baking soda, mace and salt. Add alternately, with sour cream, beginning and ending with dry ingredients. Spoon batter into prepared muffin tins. Sprinkle with cinnamon and sugar mixture. Bake at 350 degrees for 30 minutes. Contributed by Marilyn Wassink Hanson, Kohler.

H.C. Prange Shrimp Salad

1/4 cup water
1/2 cup sugar
2 cups Miracle Whip
1 pound package curly noodles
3 small cans shrimp, broken and deveined
1 10 oz. box frozen peas
1/4 cup carrots, shredded
1/2 cup celery, chopped
1/2 cup onion, chopped
1tsp. dill weed

Boil sugar and water for one minute. Cool. Cook curly noodles, drain and cool. Then add cooled sugar and water mixture to the Miracle Whip. Add shrimp, peas, carrots, celery, onion and dill weed. Toss gently. Refrigerate.

Contributed by Lois A. Anderson, Stewartville, Minnesota.

Prange's Cranberry Salad

2 packages cranberries, coarsely chopped

1 cup sugar

1 quart apple, 4 cups, finely cut

1/2 cup chopped nuts

1 package small marshmallows

1 can Dream whip

Mix cranberries, sugar, apples and nuts. Fold in whipped topping and marshmallow.

Contributed by Robert Vogt, Sheboygan

Prange's Macaroni Salad

2 1/2 lbs. elbow macaroni– boil in water until tender. Rinse cold water.

10 ounce package frozen peas. Mix in one tablespoon sugar and pinch of salt.

3 cups sliced celery

1 cup shredded carrots

1 tablespoon dry onion

2 teaspoons pimiento

7 hard cooked eggs

Dressing: 1 3/4 cups simple syrup

3/4 cup water

1 cup sugar

Boil together

1 quart mayonnaise

Mix all together

Contributed by Robert Vogt, Sheboygan

H. C. Prange Memories

H.C. Prange Memories

H.C. Prange Memories

H.C. Prange Memories

H.C. Prange Memories

H.C. Prange
Autographs

H.C. Prange
Autographs

H.C. Prange Photos

H.C. Prange Photos

www.ingramcontent.com/pod-product-compliance
Lightning Source LLC
Chambersburg PA
CBHW080341170426
43194CB00014B/2647